BYZANTIUM

TIME LIFE BOOKS ®

GREAT AGES OF MAN

THE LIFE HISTORY OF THE UNITED STATES

TIME-LIFE LIBRARY OF ART

LIFE WORLD LIBRARY

LIFE NATURE LIBRARY

LIFE SCIENCE LIBRARY

TIME READING PROGRAM

INTERNATIONAL BOOK SOCIETY

LIFE Pictorial Atlas of the World
The Epic of Man
The Wonders of Life on Earth
The World We Live In
The World's Great Religions
The LIFE Book of Christmas
LIFE's Picture History of Western Man
The LIFE Treasury of American Folklore
America's Arts and Skills
300 Years of American Painting
The Second World War
LIFE's Picture History of World War II
Picture Cook Book
LIFE Guide to Paris

GREAT AGES OF MAN

A History of the World's Cultures

BYZANTIUM

by

PHILIP SHERRARD

and

The Editors of TIME-LIFE Books

TIME INCORPORATED, NEW YORK

THE AUTHOR: Philip Sherrard, a distinguished English authority on Byzantium, received his doctorate from London University in modern Greek literature and held a research fellowship at Oxford University. His major publications include *Athos, the Mountain of Silence; Constantinople: Iconography of a Sacred City;* and *The Greek East and the Latin West*. He now lives with his Greek wife in Athens, where he has served as the Assistant Director of the British School of Archaeology.

THE CONSULTING EDITOR: Leonard Krieger, now University Professor at the University of Chicago, was formerly Professor of History at Yale; Dr. Krieger is the author of *The German Idea of Freedom* and *The Politics of Discretion*, and co-author of *History*, written in collaboration with John Higham and Felix Gilbert.

THE COVER: St. Demetrios, one of Byzantium's revered warrior saints, is pictured in a mosaic from the 11th Century Church of Hosios Loukas in Greece.

TIME-LIFE BOOKS

EDITOR
Maitland A. Edey

TEXT DIRECTOR   ART DIRECTOR
Jerry Korn   Edward A. Hamilton

CHIEF OF RESEARCH
Beatrice T. Dobie

Assistant Text Director: Harold C. Field
Assistant Art Director: Arnold C. Holeywell
Assistant Chiefs of Research:
Monica O. Horne, Martha Turner

PUBLISHER
Rhett Austell

General Manager: Joseph C. Hazen Jr.
Business Manager: John D. McSweeney
Circulation Director: Joan D. Manley
Publishing Board: Nicholas Benton,
Louis Bronzo, James Wendell Forbes

GREAT AGES OF MAN

SERIES EDITOR: Russell Bourne
Editorial Staff for *Byzantium:*
Assistant Editor: Carlotta Kerwin
Text Editors: Ogden Tanner, Betsy Frankel
Picture Editor: John Paul Porter
Designer: Norman Snyder
Assistant Designer: Ladislav Svatos
Staff Writers: John Stanton, Edmund White
Chief Researcher: Peggy Bushong
Researchers: Irene Ertugrul, Alice Baker,
Jacqueline Boël, Carole Isenberg, Frank Kendig,
Kaye Neil, Theo Pascal, Jeffrey Tarter,
Arlene Zuckerman

EDITORIAL PRODUCTION
Color Director: Robert L. Young
Assistant: James J. Cox
Copy Staff: Marian Gordon Goldman,
Barbara Hults, Dolores A. Littles
Picture Bureau: Margaret K. Goldsmith,
Joan Lynch, Barbara Sullivan
Traffic: Douglas Graham, David Wyland
Art Assistants: Anne Landry, Robert Pellegrini

Valuable aid in preparing this book was given by Dmitri Kessel, LIFE staff photographer; Doris O'Neil, Chief of the LIFE Picture Library; Peter Draz, Chief of the Time Inc. Bureau of Editorial Reference; Richard M. Clurman, Chief of the TIME-LIFE News Service; Correspondents Maria Vincenza Aloisi (Paris), Barbara Moir (London), Ann Natanson (Rome), Elisabeth Kraemer (Bonn).

CONTENTS

INTRODUCTION

What was the Byzantine empire? What was its place in history, and what was it that made it a historical unit? The reader who asks these questions will find that there are no simple answers. He will even find that, in a sense, there never was such a thing as a Byzantine empire; that had he lived, let us say in the 10th Century, in some provincial town of the so-called Byzantine empire and referred to its inhabitants as Byzantines, they would not have known what he was talking about. For in truth the expression "Byzantine empire" (derived from Byzantium, the ancient town on whose site Constantinople was built) is of comparatively modern origin, unknown to those who dwelled within the borders of the empire to which it refers. Nor would the inhabitants have understood a visitor if he had referred to them as Greeks, though the language they spoke was Greek. For them, the empire in which they lived was the Roman Empire and they were Romans.

The Byzantine empire was indeed a phase of the Roman Empire. It began with the triumph of Christianity and Constantine the Great's transfer of his capital from Rome to Byzantium early in the Fourth Century. Despite the loss of its western provinces, and its geographical restriction to those of the east, it perpetuated without a break the political structure which the Romans had fashioned. Although the Byzantine empire subsequently underwent changes which substantially altered its character, it retained much that was Roman in ideology, government and law. As a continuation of the Roman Empire it considered itself—and at times it actually was—the one empire in the world.

An impressive political organism which endured for over a thousand years, the Byzantine empire was also a great cultural unit at a time when, in a Europe broken up into numerous feudal units, intellectual activity was at a minimum. It continued without a break the culture of the ancient world as that culture had evolved following the conquests of Alexander the Great, the establishment first of the Hellenistic monarchies and then of the Roman Empire. The principal ingredients of that culture were Greek, but blended with them in the final result, the great Christian synthesis, were many Oriental elements. Christianity itself, the core of Byzantine life, was, in its most primitive form, Eastern in origin. So too, as the author notes, was the absolutism of the emperor, deriving his power from God and surrounded by ceremonial. And Eastern features of Byzantium's magnificent art—its abstract character, its flatness, its brilliant colors, its elaborate ornamentation—are everywhere apparent.

This synthesis of cultures, dominated by Christianity, Byzantium passed on to surrounding barbarians, such as the Balkan Slavs and the Russians, and so made civilized nations out of them. At the same time Byzantium preserved the great secular literature of classical antiquity which served as inspiration for the emerging Europe of the Renaissance. The cultural influence of Byzantium was worldwide.

It is with this empire, great both as a political organism and as a synthesizer and preserver of culture, that the following pages deal. If in the treatment of his subject the author is somewhat general, that is a matter dictated by the very nature of his assignment. The stimulating style in which he writes, however, should induce further study. If the reading of this book indeed does that, it will have achieved its purpose.

PETER CHARANIS

Voorhees Professor of History, Rutgers, The State University, New Jersey

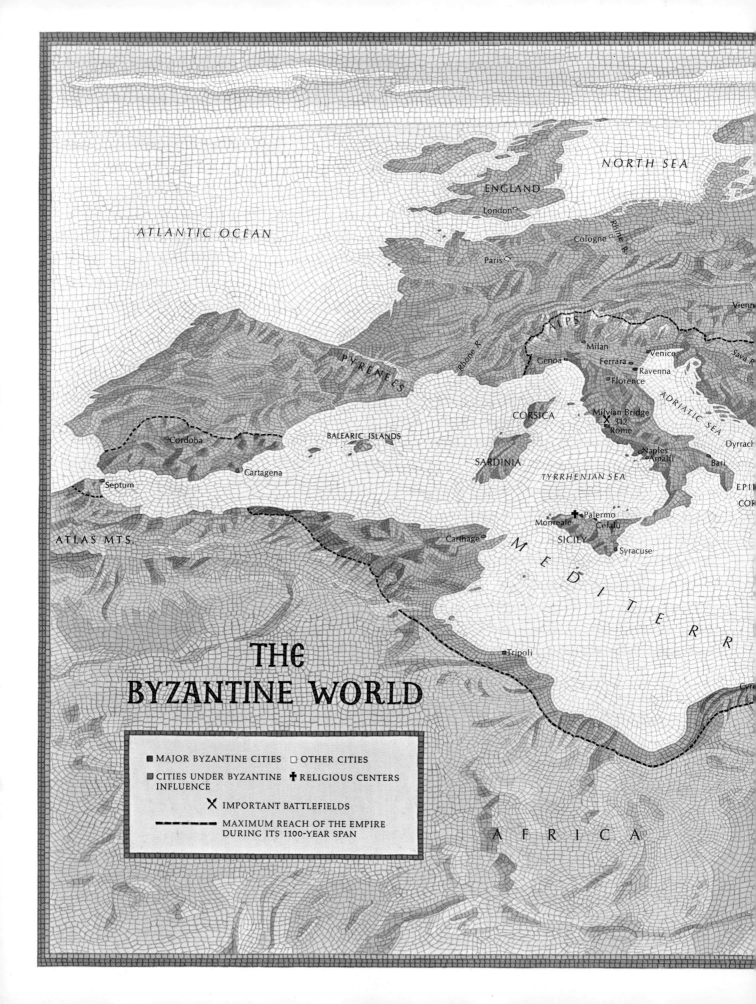

THE BYZANTINE WORLD

NORTH SEA

ATLANTIC OCEAN

ENGLAND
London

Cologne
Rhine R.
Paris

ALPS
Vienn
Milan
Venice
Genoa
Ferrara
Ravenna
Sava R
PYRENEES
Rhone R.
Florence
ADRIATIC SEA

CORSICA
Milvian Bridge
X 312
Rome
Dyrrach
BALEARIC ISLANDS
Cordoba
Naples
Amalfi
Bari
EPI
Cartagena
SARDINIA
TYRRHENIAN SEA
COR
Septum
Monreale
Palermo
Cefalù
ATLAS MTS.
Carthage
SICILY
Syracuse
M E D I T E R R
Tripoli
Cy

MAJOR BYZANTINE CITIES □ **OTHER CITIES**

CITIES UNDER BYZANTINE INFLUENCE ✝ **RELIGIOUS CENTERS**

X **IMPORTANT BATTLEFIELDS**

——————— **MAXIMUM REACH OF THE EMPIRE DURING ITS 1100-YEAR SPAN**

A F R I C A

BALTIC SEA

Novgorod

Kiev

ORAVIA

CARPATHIAN MTS.

Dnieper R.

Don R.

CASPIAN SEA

Belgrade

CRIMEA

Cherson

CAUCASUS MTS.

Danube River

Varna

BLACK SEA

ssovo
1389

Naissus

Sardica

Trebizond

Kars   Ani

id MACEDONIA

Adrianople

X 378

ARMENIA

alonika

Constantinople

Chalcedon

Heraclea

Manzikert X

✝ Mount Athos

Nicomedia

ANATOLIA
(Asia Minor)

1071

ESSALY

X Nicaea

Lake Van

teora

Brusa
1326

AEGEAN SEA

OCIS Daphni

Caesarea

egara Athens

Smyrna

CAPPADOCIA

Aistra

CHIOS

Ephesus

Edessa

PERSIA

OPONNESE PATMOS

Aleppo

RHODES

Antioch

Euphrates R.

Tigris River

Olympos

CRETE   KARPATHOS

CYPRUS

SYRIA

N E A N   S E A

Beirut

Damascus

Ctesiphon

PALESTINE

Jerusalem

Alexandria

EGYPT

ARABIA

✝ Mount Sinai

Nile River

RED SEA

David Greenspan

1

THE NEW ROME

For a long time the general view of the history of Western civilization relegated to a minor place one of the most fascinating and influential ages in the human record. It is remarkable that Byzantium, a vast empire and a brilliant cultural entity that lasted more than a thousand years, was almost disregarded by most historians of the West.

According to this general view, Western civilization had its origins in ancient Greece. Behind the ancient Greek world itself lay the impressive if sometimes shadowy forms of several other civilizations—among them Assyria and Egypt, India and Minoan Crete. But it was in ancient Greece that the vital elements of these earlier civilizations were fused into a pattern of civil and cultural life that we now recognize as specifically Western. The Greeks, however, failed to practice their political thought on any scale larger than that of the city-state. Although Alexander the Great broke through the confines of the classical Greek world and diffused Greek culture across the lands of Anatolia, Syria and Egypt, he failed to create a political organization capable of uniting the numerous peoples he had conquered.

It was only three centuries later, with the rise of Roman power and the consolidation of Roman rule, that Western civilization for the first time acquired a pattern for political order. Rome absorbed and preserved Greek culture and education within a political structure that stretched from York in Britain to Alexandria in Egypt, from the Atlantic to the Euphrates. Yet it was an Empire destined to disintegrate. After some five centuries, between the Fourth Century and the early Sixth Century, the great barbarian leaders—Alaric, Attila, Clovis, and Theodoric—swept into Italy and other parts of the empire in the West. Rome's old ruling classes were destroyed and the West sank into that period of its history known as the Dark Ages.

The next great phase in this general view of Western civilization is represented by the Renaissance, and the revival of learning and culture which took place in Italy and elsewhere from 1400 onward. The "rediscovery" of the literature and art of the ancient Greco-Roman world, hidden for so many centuries under a blanket of ignorance and

BYZANTIUM'S IMPERIAL EAGLE, *seen here on a 10th Century silk shroud, was a traditional emblem of Roman authority that craftsmen in the East preserved and imitated for centuries after the collapse of the Roman Empire.*

Α	Β	Γ	Δ	Ε	Ζ	Η	Θ	Ι
alpha	beta	gamma	delta	epsilon	zeta	eta	theta	iota

Ꙗ	ББ	Г	Ꙉ	Є	Ꙁ	И	Ѳ	I
az	buki, vedi	glagol'	dobro	yest'	zemlya	izhe	fita	i

illiteracy, brought the "dark" Middle Ages to an end and prepared the way for the emergence of the modern Western world.

In this scheme of things, there is a strange kind of gap or hiatus between the decline of the Roman Empire and the rise of Renaissance Italy. The civilized world is supposed to have suffered an eclipse. Not even the glories of Charlemagne's court and the brilliance of medieval scholarship are of any consequence. It is assumed that from 400 to 1400 A.D. the progress of the arts and sciences, and indeed all cultural life, came to a halt.

This version of history is more than an oversimplification: it is a misrepresentation. For between the old Roman Empire and the Renaissance lay the great age of Byzantium. It endured for some eleven centuries, and formed a strategic bridge between antiquity and the modern world. It not only preserved the two unifying elements of the Roman Empire—Roman law and state organization, and the inherited tradition of Hellenic culture—it added a third and even more powerful organizing force: Christianity.

Indeed, the wonder is not that Byzantium is being "rediscovered" today but that it for so long remained shrouded in mystery and misunderstanding. There is, to be sure, a sizable part of the world that does regard Byzantium as a major source of its cultural lineage—the Balkans and western Russia. To these sections of Europe more than to any others did Byzantium (which fell to the Turks in 1453) transmit its rich heritage of tradition and

invention. The Orthodox Christian religion, the Cyrillic alphabet, the very way of life of these people may be traced to Byzantine origins.

Most striking among Byzantium's unique contributions to Eastern Europe and Western Asia are its brilliant mosaics, and the architectural forms and engineering skills evident in its churches—glittering, many-faceted structures being built on the same principles in these same areas today. Wherever on the twisted ridges of Yugoslavia, in the open valleys of Romania, or on the Syrian deserts one sees the many majestic vaults and domes of a stone church, there one must also acknowledge a debt to the genius of the Byzantine builders who first developed such a hierarchy of forms.

Though indebtedness to Byzantium may be obvious in Eastern Europe, it is more subtle and more grudgingly recognized in the countries of the West. The revival of Greek ideas during the Renaissance would have been largely impossible had not Byzantine scholars studied and preserved the ancient literature. Certain cathedrals from the reign of Charlemagne, like the one still standing at Aachen in Germany, use Byzantine decorative motifs, floor plans and construction techniques; but these are generally counted as features of Carolingian art. And it is a forgotten bit of cultural history that the fork—that most characteristic implement of Western table service—was first introduced to Venetian society by a Byzantine princess.

Indeed, in the eyes of many Westerners, the Byzantines have continued to seem either like his-

Κ	Λ	Μ	Ν	Ξ	Ο	Π	Ρ	Σ	Τ	Υ	Φ	Χ	Ψ	Ω
kappa	lambda	mu	nu	xi	omicron	pi	rho	sigma	tau	upsilon	phi	chi	psi	omega
К	Л	М	Н	Ѯ	О	П	Р	С	Т	V	Ф	Х	Ѱ	Ѡ
kako	lyudi	myslete	nash	ksi	on	pokoi	rtsy	slovo	tvyordo	izhita	fert	kha	psi	omega

torical nonentities, or like grotesque figures in a strange and tasteless drama. Perhaps this is because of the Byzantine's great passion for three aspects of life that have always been rather suspect in the West: spectacular popular circuses, courtly intrigue (including royal eye-gougings) and religious mysticism. Shocked, puzzled or dismayed by a long chronicle of activities in these three spheres, such writers as the Englishman William Lecky have concluded that Byzantium was merely "a monotonous story of the intrigues of priests, eunuchs and women, of poisonings, of conspiracies, of uniform ingratitude, of perpetual fratricide."

Byzantine life may have had its strange and even grisly side, but its underlying pattern, as we are now beginning to see, was one of surprising beauty, consistency and, above all, durability. Furthermore, it possessed sufficient power and glory to bind together virtually all of the nonbarbarian world before the rise of the West, thus demonstrating an admirable mastery of men and events. If only for this reason it is necessary to attempt a more deeply penetrating view of Byzantium. And to understand Byzantine civilization, it is necessary to examine the main forces that forged it: the changing form of the Roman Empire and the rise of Christianity.

By the second half of the Third Century, the Roman Empire founded by Augustus scarcely 300 years before faced disintegration. Augustus' imperial system had been a masterpiece. At the time of his succession to power, Rome was the focal point of the Western world; all eyes turned to it. Some looked to Rome for protection and leadership; some watched it apprehensively, fearing new demands upon their territory or authority. But despite this commanding position, the Roman state was in turmoil. Still governed by a system suitable to a city, not an empire, it was wracked by internal strife. While preserving the governmental forms of the Republic, Augustus succeeded in creating a strong authoritarian government that recognized both the needs of empire and the age-old Roman dislike for autocracy and kingship.

At its inception, the Augustan system was surprisingly farsighted. But by the Third Century the empire had been brought close to the breaking point by a combination of factors—misuse of authority, bureaucratic bumbling, a foundering economy, civil wars, barbarian raids and the private scheming of ambitious men. The political climate of the times was demonstrated as early as the year 193, when a popular emperor, Pertinax, was murdered by the elite Praetorian Guard, which then proceeded to auction off the emperorship. The winner was one Julianus, a wealthy senator who, according to a contemporary account, "was holding a drinking bout late that evening [when] his wife and daughters and fellow feasters urged him to rise from his banqueting couch and hasten to the barracks . . . on the way they pressed it on him that he might get the sovereignty for himself and that he ought not to spare the money to outbid any competitors . . ." The Roman Empire was his.

Within months, however, Julianus had himself

been deposed and murdered, and by 235 A.D. military anarchy had set in. In the next 50 years there were 20 legitimate emperors in addition to uncounted usurpers who ruled sections of the Empire at various times. The concept of central government became a mockery: power was in the hands of the provincial armies whose loyalties were to their own commanders, not to the Empire. In the West, a general named Postumus seized Gaul and some of Spain and ruled these provinces as a separate kingdom for nine years. In the East, a woman named Zenobia, widow of a Palmyran prince, conquered the Roman provinces of Asia Minor and even extended her influence into Egypt, the breadbasket of the Empire. Though eventually defeated by Emperor Aurelian, her contempt for Rome, which had once held undisputed sway over virtually the whole known world, is revealed in this reply to Aurelian's demand for surrender:

"The Persians do not abandon us, and we will await their succors. The Saracens and the Armenians are on our side. The brigands of Syria have defeated your army, O Aurelian . . . what will it be when we have received the reinforcements which come to us from all sides? You will lower then that tone with which you,—as if already full conqueror—now bid me to surrender."

The men who came to power on the strength of their armies failed, almost without exception, to find effective solutions to the administrative and economic chaos at home. The silver coinage had been severely debased—at one point it was 95 per cent copper—and more and more worthless money was minted in a vain attempt to meet the rising tide of inflation. The sophisticated economy collapsed into a system of payment in kind; soldiers and civil servants were paid in rations and clothing. Repeated wars and repeated waves of the plague depleted manpower to such a degree that large tracts of land passed from cultivated acreage to wild land.

Provincial town magistrates who were responsible for collecting taxes were required to fulfill their quotas to the state even though the land lay idle without men or money to work it; these once-honored government positions became a heavy burden which had to be forced upon the citizens. The Roman Empire had become a top-heavy bureaucracy, always demanding more men, more goods, more taxes from provinces almost wrung dry.

Into this scene stepped a Dalmatian soldier, Diocletian, a powerful personality who openly advocated a system of autocratic power. He successfully asserted the concept of the divine right of the emperor and, armed with this power, he systematically set about restoring order to the crumbling Empire. First, he fortified the frontiers against the threat of force from outlying barbarians and separated civil authority from the military to forestall violent military coups from within. He also made attempts to fix the value of coinage and issued his famous Price Edict, which established a maximum price for goods and wages, category by category, throughout the Empire; though not wholly successful, these steps did arrest the momentum of the downhill spiral of the economy.

Diocletian also recognized the unwieldiness of Rome's far-flung bureaucracy and carved its provinces into smaller units, almost doubling their number and thereby weakening the power of provincial governors to contest the Emperor's authority. The provinces were grouped into dioceses and these in turn were organized into four prefectures. At the top, Diocletian split the administration between two emperors, each with the title of Augustus— one in the East and one in the West. To control the matter of orderly succession, each emperor had an heir apparent with the title of Caesar. Each was responsible for a given area of the Empire; but all decrees of government had to be issued in the name of all four members of the tetrarchy.

OLD AND NEW CAPITALS *of the Roman Empire are personified by female figures in the Fifth Century ivory plaques at right. Rome (left) wears a military helmet; Constantinople's crown symbolizes the walls of her city.*

Diocletian himself took the post of emperor in the East, choosing as his capital Nicomedia, not far from the city which was soon to become Constantinople. Here, his use of the divine status of the emperor, in itself an Eastern concept, took on oriental trappings and ceremonies: he put a diadem on his head, scarlet buskins on his feet and had himself clad in robes of purple by the eunuchs who attended him in the inner sanctuary of his court. He claimed descent from Jupiter, king of the gods, and when he revealed himself in audience those who came before him had to prostrate themselves in adoration.

The steps Diocletian took to check the disintegration of the Roman Empire indirectly set the stage for the rise of Byzantium. For in preserving the Empire, Diocletian also revitalized it and gave new importance to the Eastern dominions. The sound new substructure that underlay the Roman state would become the Byzantine empire. Yet there

was another force within the Empire—a force which Diocletian failed to utilize or even to cope with—which helped create Byzantium. That force was Christianity.

In Diocletian's time, the religion that was to play so important a role in Byzantine civilization was spreading throughout the Empire despite innumerable obstacles. The moral and spiritual standards of Christians often brought them into conflict with Roman law, calling down on them persecutions so harsh that the persistence of early Christianity often seems amazing. Not the least of Christianity's obstacles was the multitude of religions and philosophies that vied for the loyalties of the peoples of the Roman world. Two of Christianity's strongest competitors were the pagan philosophies, Stoicism and Neoplatonism.

Stoicism, with its ideal of an ordered society and its strictly practical morality, appealed to the Roman mind, which ranked practical efficiency high among

15

the virtues. When, two centuries after the birth of Christ, the Emperor, Marcus Aurelius, adopted Stoicism as his guiding philosophy, it reached its zenith.

Neoplatonism, claiming descent from some of the more spiritual aspects of Plato's doctrines, had its origins in Roman Alexandria. Unlike Stoicism, its appeal was not solely to reason, but to the desire for a mystical experience of an Absolute beyond the grasp of rational thought. Its highly speculative and contemplative nature prevented it from having extensive popular appeal. It appealed to the few, to those capable of mastering its complex metaphysical structure. Neither Stoicism nor Neoplatonism held out anything for the poor in spirit, for the multitude of slaves at the bottom of Greek and Roman society, or for those who labored and were heavy laden.

For those great masses of the people some leavening of the frustrations and hardships of life was provided by various "mystery" religions. The Romans were willing to tolerate any cult provided it did not run counter to the interests of the state or promote civil disturbance. Hence they permitted the existence within the Roman system of the numerous cults of North Africa and the East, religions with exotic gods and bizarre rites. One of the most ubiquitous of these cults was Mithraism, whose masculine nature and worship of Apollo, the unconquered Sun, made it particularly popular among soldiers. But none of the mystery cults had an appeal strong and universal enough to provide on a spiritual plane what Roman law provided on the plane of civil organization and what Greek classical tradition provided on the plane of culture.

Christianity was originally regarded by the Romans as just one more mystery religion, a local variant of Judaism. Thus, like Judaism, which had a working agreement with Rome and was permitted to function without hindrance, Christianity, too, was tolerated.

And so in this brief, early period of peace the teachings of Christ began to make their way through the Roman Empire. Unknowingly, the Empire aided it in other ways as well. Greek and Latin, the common languages of the Roman world, were also the languages of Christianity. And the Roman network of towns and roads, designed to facilitate government and trade, eased the task of spreading the Christian Word. Unlike the Jews, who abhorred Gentiles and held themselves aloof from the Gentile world, Christians reached out into that world. Starting as groups of local communicants who gathered to commemorate the Last Supper and who were loosely bound by a belief in the imminent Second Coming of Christ, the Christians gradually took on some of the administrative patterns of the Roman state and created an efficient religious organization of their own.

Slowly, almost imperceptibly, the new Christian Church developed its own ritual and doctrine, assimilating much from the religions and philosophies of the varied peoples of the Empire. Its leading thinkers and intellectuals—Irenaeus, Origen, Clement of Alexandria—took over the language and many of the ideas of Greek philosophy. Many of its customs and services were based on the Judaic forms, but Christians also adopted rituals and even dates from pagan religions. (The date of Christmas, for example, was pegged at December 25 to compete with a Mithraitic festival day, although the exact date of Christ's birth was not, and is not, known.) Thus Christianity added to its other strengths a universal appeal. By the Third Century it was well on its way to becoming the most powerful single force within the Empire, capable of infusing new life into Rome's failing governmental structure and the weakening tradition of classical learning.

During the early years of their existence, Christians had not been in actual conflict with the state.

When confronted with the choice of submission or suffering, they consistently chose the second. They had no desire to thwart imperial authority, but when they were required by Diocletian to accept the concept of the emperor as a god, and to worship him, they refused. Diocletian countered by embarking on what was to be the last great persecution of Rome's Christian subjects, thereby missing the chance to harness this dynamic element for the benefit of the Empire. In 303 he issued the first of a series of edicts, ordering churches to be razed, sacred books to be burned, and Christians themselves to be enslaved, imprisoned or tortured if they refused to give up their faith.

Diocletian's edicts made martyrs out of some of the victims, and impressed more than one pagan Roman with the extent of Christian courage. The hour for Christianity's triumph had not yet struck, but it was not to be delayed for very long. In 305 Diocletian voluntarily abdicated. His re-formed empire, lacking any integrating force such as Christianity might have provided, barely survived him. By 311 there were four rulers claiming the title of emperor. One of them, stationed in the West, was Constantine.

Constantine was born in Moesia, the Roman province which became the home of the Serbs and the Bulgars. His father Constantius was one of Diocletian's governors in the West and later became one of the Western co-emperors; his mother was Helena, later St. Helena, a Christian lady and former serving maid who reputedly found and dug up the true Cross of Christ in Palestine. As a youth, Constantine was sent to Diocletian's court at Nicomedia and later served in the army in Persia and Egypt. When Diocletian retired, Constantine joined his father in Britain. There, as a young general in the Roman army, he became his father's successor, and was acclaimed Augustus by his own troops on his father's death in 306.

HARD DAYS FOR CHRISTIANITY

St. Domninus, shown above being clubbed to death by a Roman soldier, was one of countless Christians martyred in pre-Byzantine times. Major phases in the persecutions they endured appear below.

64-67   ACCUSED BY NERO *of burning Rome, Christians are sentenced to death in the arena and at the burning stake.*

110-210   EXECUTIONS INCREASE *as the state stigmatizes Christianity as a crime.*

225-235   A PERIOD OF RESPITE *gives the followers the right to worship once more.*

235-238   RENEWED PUNISHMENTS, *including exile and death, are directed at the clergy as propagators of the faith.*

249-251   AN EMPIRE-WIDE DRIVE *against Christians is ordered by Emperor Decius.*

260-303   A SECOND RESPITE *under Gallienus permits worshipers to live unharmed.*

303-311   CHURCH-BURNINGS *mark the last of the great anti-Christian campaigns.*

311-   GALERIUS' EDICT *gives Christians the right to practice their religion and to rebuild their churches unmolested.*

Six years later Constantine defeated Maxentius, his co-emperor in the West, after a brilliant campaign that brought him to the outskirts of Rome. After reportedly seeing a heavenly vision during this campaign, Constantine declared his preference for Christianity. One year after his victory over Maxentius he defeated the Eastern Emperor, Maximum, and in 323 came his final triumph; he defeated and captured the other Eastern Emperor, Licinius, after a struggle into which both parties threw all their strength. Constantine was left sole Emperor of Rome.

Faced now with the task of arresting the disintegration of the Empire, and of welding its homogeneous parts into a durable whole, Constantine made two major decisions. First, he assured Christianity legal status within the Empire. Christian priests were allowed the same tax exemption as were those of other religions, and Christian holy days were honored as respectfully as pagan festivals. Constantine himself, who had a typically Roman enthusiasm for bricks and mortar, built many churches and encouraged bishops and wealthy civilians to do likewise. He had his children instructed in the Christian faith, and if he did not actually become a Christian himself until just before his death, this was apparently not from want of spiritual commitment. Either he thought it expedient for the Emperor to remain officially neutral, or he thought that baptism's remission of sins might as well be saved for the last moment, so that he might leave the world with a clean slate.

Constantine's other important decision was to move the Empire's capital from Rome, the scene of plot and counterplot, treason and conspiracy. To the north and west the Empire's provincial capitals were too remote and uncivilized to serve as suitable nerve centers for the vast Roman realm, but to the east lay an urban civilization older and richer than Rome's. It was also to the east that the Empire confronted its most formidable enemies—the Germanic tribes massed along the Danube and the Persians in Anatolia. There, too, the main trade routes converged; and there, finally, lay some of the most important centers of the Christian religion.

Among these cities was Jerusalem, scene of Christ's death and resurrection, an ancient capital in which Constantine authorized the building of several churches. There was Naissus, Constantine's birthplace in what is now Serbia; there was Nicomedia, whose importance as a citadel on the Anatolian frontier Diocletian had magnified by the construction of several imperial buildings; there was Sardica (Sophia), already a bustling center of trade on the way from central Europe to the Black Sea; and there was Thessalonica (Salonika), visited by St. Paul, and a city vital to the commerce of the Empire in the eastern Mediterranean. All these Constantine considered for his new imperial city, and ultimately rejected.

His thoughts also turned to Troy, ancient Ilium, scene of the epic battle between the Greeks and Trojans immortalized by Homer. Journeying to that honored site in Asia Minor he declared it a proper location for his future capital. According to legend, he personally laid out the lines of the city walls and ordered workmen to begin construction at once. But, as the story goes, the work was well under way, and the gates in the main wall had already been hung, when one night God appeared to the Emperor and commanded that he seek out yet another site for the new Rome.

Whether by divine intervention, or simply by completing his process of selection, the Emperor ultimately passed over Troy and chose Byzantium, a small trading town on a magnificently strategic site jutting into the sea of Marmara. It was one of the most momentous decisions in the history of Western civilization.

IN A DREAM *(top) Constantine is told to fight under the Cross; when he did so (below) and won, he espoused Christianity.*

PRESERVING A HERITAGE

Byzantium was both the last direct heir to the Roman Empire and the first Christian nation. Its dual nature was dramatized by Constantine himself, its founding emperor, when he erected a column in Constantinople and enclosed in its base a statue of Athena and baskets said to have held the bread Christ fed his disciples. Throughout its long history, Byzantium remained faithful both to its classical heritage and to its Christian precepts. The imperial court discussed Greek philosophy and recited Homer, but it also sent missionaries to the Near East and converted the Russians. The Byzantines systematized Roman law and patterned their Senate after Rome's, yet supported hundreds of monasteries and sought the political advice of mystics. Typically, the 11th Century ruler Irene Ducas styled herself "Empress of the Romans—faithful in Christ our Lord."

JUSTINIAN THE JURIST *stands with churchmen and officials of his court during Communion service. Though a powerful autocrat, Justinian believed tha*

THE CODIFICATION OF ROMAN LAW

One of the greatest Byzantine contributions to Western civilization was the clarification and transmission of the essence of Roman law. The Romans had bequeathed to Byzantium a vast body of legal opinion that was frequently antiquated or contradictory. Justinian, the great Sixth Century Emperor, reduced this tangled collection to a coherent system. In 528 A.D. he appointed a commission of 10 men who classified the constitutions written by various Roman emperors into a single code of 4,652 laws. Another commission produced a

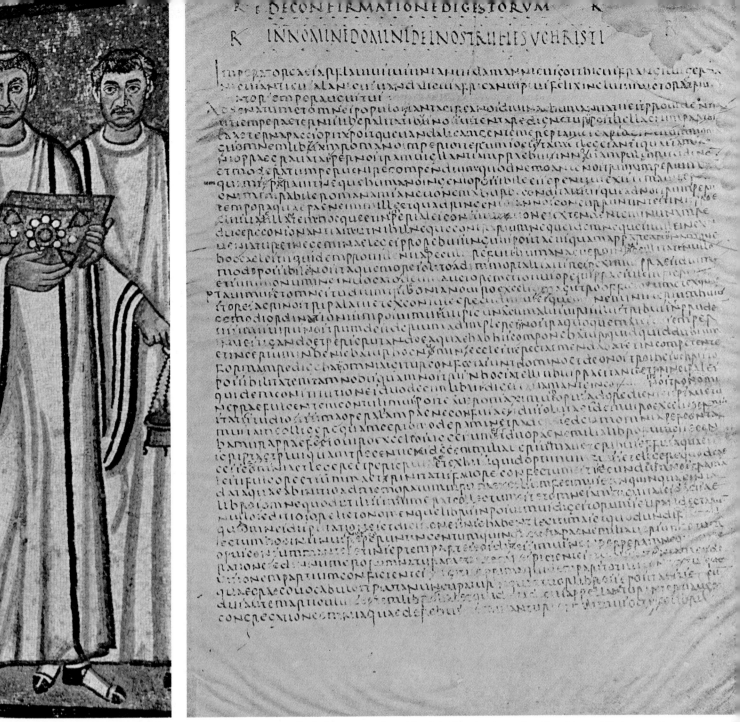

imperial authority should submit to law.   AN INTRODUCTION *to a Sixth Century version of Justinian's code summarizes the virtues of the new system.*

50-volume digest of major decisions that had been handed down by authoritative jurists in the Second and Third Centuries, the golden age of Roman law.

In civil law, the new system was more efficient and progressive than the ancient Roman statutes it supplanted. Justinian made it easier, for example, to free slaves and to sell land. He also guaranteed the inheritance rights of widows and reduced the absolute power of fathers over the lives of their children.

In the area of criminal law, however, the new system was far sterner than its predecessor. The Christian jurists for the first time made crimes out of heresy and seduction. Heretics who varied from Orthodox practice were barred from holding office and denied their inheritance. A seducer was automatically executed, as was his victim if she willingly submitted; if the girl's chaperone encouraged the alliance, molten lead was poured in her mouth. Despite such barbaric provisions, Justinian's code was so clear and consistent that it later served as the model for the legal systems of most European nations.

AN ARCHITECTURAL PROTOTYPE, *Constantinople's Church of the Holy Apostles (seen here in a 12th Century illumination) inspired Venice's Church of St. Mark.*

THE SWEEPING EFFECT
OF BYZANTINE ART

In the realm of art, Byzantium served both as a curator and as an innovator. The Byzantines preserved many of the glories of Greek and Roman sculpture, such as the Greek horses of gilded bronze *(right)*. As innovators, they developed a style of religious art and architecture that influenced every nation they encountered. In Italy, which was part of the Eastern empire until the Seventh Century, they built churches in Rome, Milan, Ravenna and Naples and virtually an entire Byzantine city in Venice. The Bulgarians and Serbians carefully copied well-known Byzantine churches and palaces, and the Russians laid out important towns in imitation of Constantinople. The Persians respected Byzantine taste so much that one of their rulers pulled down his new palace when an envoy from the emperor remarked of the building, "The upper part will do for birds and the lower for rats."

A MOSAIC IN ST. MARK'S, *depicting the exterior of the church, shows its obvious debt to its Byzantine model (far left). The churchmen and citizens in front are honoring the relics of St. Mark, being borne aloft in the coffin at center.*

SCULPTURED HORSES, *which once adorned Constantinople's Hippodrome, now stand in front of St. Mark's. The horses were the pride of the Byzantine capital until the 13th Century, when Crusaders carried them off to Western Europe.*

RELICS OF A NATION RULED BY CHRIST

The Byzantines regarded themselves as the chosen people of God. Their capital of Constantinople was filled with holy relics of the saints and of the Passion and was dedicated to the Virgin, whom the people revered as the city's spiritual guardian against all enemies. In the Imperial Palace the Four Gospels were placed on an empty throne as a symbol of the living presence of God. The emperor claimed to rule by divine right and to serve as the spokesman of Heaven's will; at his coronation a chorus sang, "Glory to God who made you emperor." To dramatize his role, he occasionally mounted the pulpit and preached a sermon to the court. Artists always portrayed him in mosaics with a halo around his head. But the state, founded by Constantine under the Cross, kept its perspective: Christ's portrait was engraved on Byzantine coins and stamped with the motto, "Jesus Christ, King of Rulers."

THREE PILGRIMS *marvel at purported relics of Christ's Passion prized by churches in Constantinople. In the church at the center are two nails and the spear that pierced Christ's side; at the right is the Crown of Thorns.*

A JEWELED CROSS, *which was presented by the Emperor Justin II to the Vatican in the Sixth Century, contains in its center medallion a splinter that the Byzantines believed to have come from the Cross of Christ in Jerusalem.*

A COMMUNITY OF MONKS *works and meditates in cave dwellings in Syria.*

HOLY GROTTOES, *once the home of Byzantine ascetics, honeycomb the crags*

RIGOROUS TRADITIONS OF MONASTIC LIFE

Monastic orders and Christian mysticism flourished in the Byzantine world. "He who loses his life for My sake will find it," Christ had taught, and early monks interpreted Him faithfully. The first famous monk was St. Anthony, a Fourth Century hermit who shut himself up in a tomb for 20 years

...at rise up eerily out of the plain in Cappadocia. The region, part of present-day Turkey, was the first place in Asia Minor where Orthodox monks lived.

in Egypt (which was part of the empire until 650). His austere example was followed by other hermits, who flocked to him to form the first monastic community. Soon monasticism spread over Asia Minor and Greece, and by the Fifth Century it had taken root in Western Europe. Lives of great monks became the most widely read books in Byzantium, and by the middle of the Sixth Century there were 85 monasteries in Constantinople alone. Living in cities, in caves, in deserts and on remote islands, these followers of Christ spoke out fearlessly for their principles and served as the conscience of the empire.

27

BYZANTINE MISSIONARIES, *witnessed by the King and Queen of Bulgaria, baptize a convert in an illumination from a Slavic text.*

PASSING CIVILIZATION TO THE WORLD

In the view of many historians, Byzantium's greatest achievement was the civilizing influence it exerted over the peoples it encountered. As early as the Sixth Century, monks from Constantinople were seeking to penetrate such distant places as Nubia in southern Egypt. But perhaps the Byzantines' greatest success as missionaries of Christianity and civilization came 300 years later in the Slavic regions of Eastern Europe.

In 863 the King of Moravia asked the Emperor Michael III for a teacher who could preach the Christian faith to his subjects in their own language. A Byzantine monk named Cyril evolved a Slavic alphabet and set out to convert the Moravians. Although his attempts with them failed, his followers succeeded among the Bulgarians. By the 10th Century other countries, including Russia, had joined the Orthodox fold, and Cyril's written language eventually became, in modified forms, the basis for the culture of the entire Slavic world.

A FRESCO IN NUBIA, *from one of 60 churches that were built there by Byzantin*

...chitects, shows the archangel Michael holding a cross and spreading his peacock wings to protect Shadrach, Meshach and Abed-nego in the fiery furnace.

2
CONSTANTINE'S CITY

EMPEROR AND BUILDER, *a haloed Constantine holds a symbolic model of the city he dedicated in 330 A.D. He enclosed vast tracts of empty land within its walls, but by 413 Constantinople's boundaries had to be enlarged.*

Nearly a thousand years before Constantine decided to make his new capital a Christian city located in the East, a Greek colonizer named Byzas sailed northeast from his home at Megara across the Aegean. He passed the site of Troy, then sailed into the Dardanelles and across the Sea of Marmara. Then he came to the entrance of the Bosporus, the narrow channel that winds for some 17 miles between a double range of shrub-covered and rocky hills to emerge, at last, into the Black Sea.

Before he set sail, Byzas asked the Delphic Oracle where to establish his new colonial city. In its usual ambiguous manner, the Oracle told him: "Opposite the blind." Only when he reached the Bosporus did Byzas realize what the Oracle meant: on the Asiatic shore, opposite the hill-tipped, triangular peninsula that terminated the European land mass, earlier Greek colonists had already founded a city, Chalcedon. It was they who must have been blind not to have noticed the obvious superiority of the site lying half a mile or so away on the opposite shore. It was here that Byzas founded his own city, which took its name from him. Byzantium it was to be called until Constantine the Great made it his capital. He called it New Rome, but later it became known as Constantinople, City of Constantine. Byzas' name was to live on in history as the modern appellation of the imperial civilization which Constantine established.

The City of Constantine stood on a beautiful site that had natural defenses and commercial advantages. It dominated the north-south sea route from Russia to the Mediterranean. Along this route, from the ports of southern Russia and from the Danube, across the Black Sea, and through the Bosporus, ships would carry corn and furs, caviar and salt, honey and gold, wax and slaves. From the south, from the rich gardens of Anatolia and granaries of Egypt would come food to feed the city's growing population.

Constantinople stood where the land routes from Asia to Eastern Europe found their narrowest sea crossing. So to and through Constantinople, from places as distant as India, Ceylon and China, would be carried ivory and amber, porcelain and precious stones, silks and damask; aloes and balsam, cinnamon and sugar, musk and ginger, and many other

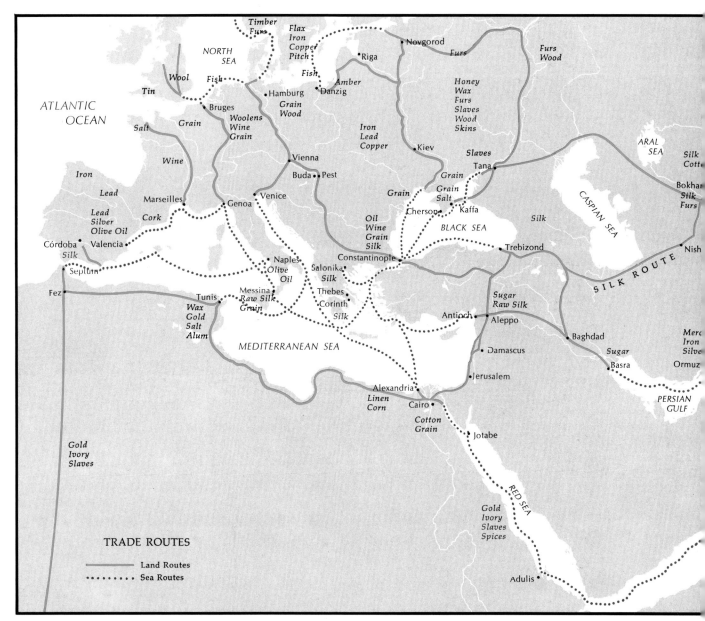

BYZANTIUM'S TRADE ROUTES linked three continents in a network of caravan tracks, rivers, seaways and Roman-style paved roads. The empire controlled only a part of these routes, yet Byzantine merchants imported products from as far away as Iceland, Ethiopia, northern Russia, Ceylon and China. Even in times of peace, goods passed through many hands along the way. A cargo of spices from the Indies, for example, required Persian and Abyssinian dhows to transport it across the Indian Ocean, Byzantine merchantmen to bring it up the Red Sea to Jotabe and Suez, a caravan to carry it overland to Alexandria, and still other ships to take it across the Mediterranean. The center of almost all commerce was Constantinople, which prospered by receiving, refining and re-exporting the goods that passed through its markets. Eventually, however, Moslem invasions disrupted many of Byzantium's lifelines—and after the empire fell Portuguese explorers succeeded in charting an easier all-sea passage around Africa to the Orient.

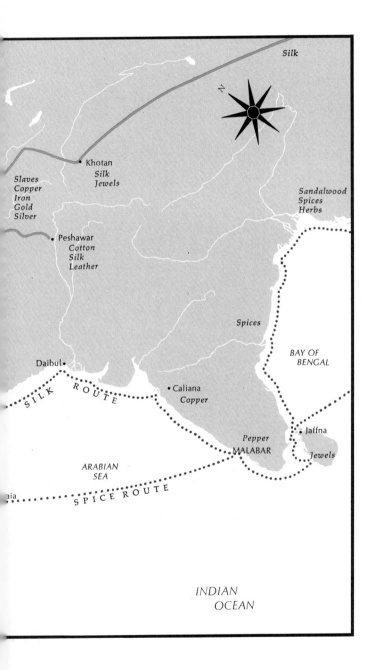

Silk

Khotan
Silk
Jewels

Slaves
Copper
Iron
Gold
Silver

Sandalwood
Spices
Herbs

Peshawar
Cotton
Silk
Leather

Spices

Daibul

BAY OF
BENGAL

SILK ROUTE

Caliana
Copper

Jaffna

Pepper
MALABAR

Jewels

ARABIAN
SEA

SPICE ROUTE

...aia

INDIAN
OCEAN

spices and medicaments. West of the city lay other fertile districts where grapes and grains flourished, and the waters of the Bosporus and the Sea of Marmara, which lapped at the city's shoreline, teemed with fish.

The defenses that nature bestowed on the city were impressive. To the south stretched the Sea of Marmara, and almost at the point where the Bosporus flowed into this sea a narrow inlet leads along the northern shore of the triangular peninsula to form a perfect landlocked harbor. This is the Golden Horn, named for its shape and the wealth that the commerce of the world deposited on its docks. As the Sixth Century Byzantine writer Procopius observed, the Horn "is always calm, being made by nature never to be stormy, as though limits were set to the billows and the surge was shut out in the city's honor. And in winter when harsh winds fall upon the sea and the strait [the Bosporus], as soon as ships reach the bay's entrance, they can proceed without pilot and moor easily. The whole bay is about five miles long and all of it is a harbor, so that when a ship anchors there the stern rides on the sea while the prow rests on land, as if the two elements rivaled each other in their desire to be of greatest service to the city."

When Constantine decided to move the capital from Rome, he also decided to make his new capital another Rome, if possible more magnificent than the old one. Like Rome, Constantinople was a "city of the seven hills," and like Rome the city was divided into 14 districts. From the old Rome Constantine brought the sacred talisman of the Roman Empire, the Palladium, the wooden statue of Pallas Athena believed to have dropped from the sky and to have been carried by Aeneas from Troy to Italy. He also brought from the ancient capital members of noble families to form a new senatorial class, and he established them in fine houses.

The main imperial buildings were constructed on Roman models. All the statues and other works of ancient art Constantine could lay hands on he transferred to his city. Among them were such masterpieces as the so-called Calydonian boar and the serpentine column from Delphi on which had been inscribed the names of the Greek cities which defeated the Persians at Plateia in 479 B.C.

In one vital respect, Constantinople was not an imitation of old Rome, for it was to be a Christian city. Constantine began the building of Hagia Sophia (the Church of Holy Wisdom) and completed many others, including the Church of the Holy Apostles. At the latter, among the 12 symbolic tombs of the apostles, he placed a 13th tomb—his own. Here also many later emperors were buried, for all the Byzantine emperors were regarded as "the equal of the apostles."

Throughout his new city Constantine introduced Christian emblems such as crosses and relics of the saints. Other objects connected with the new faith—the adze with which Noah was supposed to have built the ark, the spikenard with which Mary Magdalen was said to have anointed the feet of Christ—Constantine immured at the foot of a huge column. This column, made up of six large drums of porphyry carved with encircling laurel leaves, was set up at the center of a magnificent elliptical forum, paved with marble and surrounded with colonnades. This was the Forum of Constantine.

Over the years, monuments, memorials and holy objects connected with the Christian faith multiplied throughout the city. A great many were specifically associated with the Virgin Mary, who was considered to be the city's special protectress. "You would not find any public place or imperial dwelling, no reputable inn or private house of those in authority where there was not a church or an oratory of the Mother of God," it was later said by a student of the period. In a church at the northwest extremity of the landward walls, on a site known as Blachernae, was kept one of the most precious of all the city's relics, the Virgin's robe, which had been brought to Constantinople from Palestine at the time of Leo I (457-474). Here too was a miraculous icon of the Virgin, covered by a veil which, it was said, sometimes mysteriously parted to disclose the image beneath.

At another church dedicated to Mary lay her belt, a relic that had produced a host of miracles. At times of great peril, such as the many sieges the city endured, these relics and icons of the Virgin played a most vital part. During an attack by the Russians in 860, when the city was deprived of all hope, the Virgin's robe was carried round the walls and battlements, and the Russians abandoned the siege.

"Truly," a contemporary witness, the Patriarch Photius, wrote, "is this most holy garment the robe of God's Mother! It embraced the walls, and the foes inexplicably showed their backs; the city put it around itself, and the camp of the enemy was broken up as at a signal; the city bedecked itself with it, and the enemy were deprived of the hopes that bore them on. For immediately as the Virgin's robe went round the walls, the barbarians gave up the siege and broke camp, while we were delivered from impending capture and were granted unexpected salvation."

Relics were brought to the capital from all parts of the Christian world. They reposed in churches, sanctuaries and shrines, encased in gold and silver, ornamented with precious stones, often wrapped in a cloth of silk. The city became an enormous reliquary. Here was the linen worn by the Infant Jesus, here was the blood-covered mantle worn by Christ on the Cross, the lance that pierced His side, the Crown of Thorns, and the stone of the Tomb; here reposed the venerated relics of the Apostles St. Luke and St. Andrew, and of St. Paul's compan-

A REVERED RELIC, *contained in a casket held by the two church-men at left, is carried in a procession through the city as the people look on. The scene is on a Sixth Century ivory plaque, itself thought to have been part of a Byzantine reliquary casket.*

ion, St. Timothy, and the head of John the Baptist.

The official beginning of all this dates from May 11, 330, the day of the city's inauguration. On that day a statue of Apollo—the head of which had been replaced by a head of Constantine—was hoisted to the top of the column in the Forum. The statue of Constantine-Apollo, bearing in its right hand a scepter and in its left hand a globe representing the world, survived until the opening years of the 12th Century, when it fell in a storm and was replaced by a golden cross.

Constantine's building activities were formidable. Using marble brought from islands in the Sea of Marmara, and wood from the forests bordering the Black Sea, he enlarged the Hippodrome, which had been built by Septimus Severus a little over a century before. A list compiled a century or so later included among the city's edifices at the time two theaters, eight public and 153 private baths (including the famous Baths of Zeuxippus, also begun earlier), 52 porticoes, five granaries, eight

aqueducts or cisterns, 14 churches, 14 palaces, and 4,388 houses of sufficient size to be recorded.

Under the pressure of the growing populace, the area of the city swelled to take in another slice of land stretching between the Golden Horn and the Sea of Marmara. In the Fifth Century, to defend this enlargement on the landward side, a huge triple line of walls, three miles in length, was built. Their remains can still be seen. Earlier walls had been built along the shore of the Sea of Marmara and along the Golden Horn, so that the city became virtually an enclosed fortress.

The greatest change in the physical appearance of Constantinople took place in the Sixth Century, when some of the greatest architectural glories of the Byzantine world were built under the Emperor Justinian. The opportunity, and necessity, for a great spate of building was provided in 532 by riots followed by a fire that burned for five days and razed half the original city to the ground. Many of the main public buildings erected by Constantine and his successors—including the central church, Hagia Sophia—were destroyed.

Justinian rapidly had the rubble and charred remains of gutted buildings cleared away. Summoning the greatest architects he could find—Isidore of Miletus and Anthemius of Tralles were two of the most important—he set to work with what seemed like superhuman energy to repair the damage. Justinian set the seal of imperial magnificence on the city. He completely reconstructed Hagia Sophia and undertook a vast public building program. Later emperors made further contributions, such as enlarging the imperial palace, erecting yet another church, embellishing a forum, laying out a public garden. But in its main features, the city was as Justinian left it down to the time of its capture by the Turks in 1453.

That the city presented a spectacular sight we know from the comments of later travelers. "O what a splendid city," Fulk of Chartres was to exclaim in the 11th Century, "how stately, how fair, how many monasteries therein, how many palaces raised by sheer labor in its broadways and streets, how many works of art, marvelous to behold; it would be wearisome to tell of the abundance of all good things; of gold and of silver, garments of manifold fashion, and such sacred relics. Ships are at all times putting in at this port, so that there is nothing that men want that is not brought hither." At that period, the Golden Horn was the anchorage for barks of Dalmatians or Croats, caiques from the Greek islands, the high galleys of Genoa, Venice or Amalfi, light feluccas from the east, and the big dromonds of the imperial Byzantine fleet, equipped with tubes for projecting the mysterious "Greek fire," the secret weapon of the Byzantines.

Inside the great walls surrounding the city were a few thoroughfares and a dense tangle of narrow streets. Many of these lanes could not accommodate a sizable cart and so goods were usually carried by camels, mules, or on the backs of men. It was common to see a man—or even a child—bent over horizontal from the waist to support a heavy load strapped to his back. It was often cheaper and simpler to hire a man to transport something than to have an animal do the job. The streets too were filled with the singsong call of peddlers offering various commodities and merchants who went from house to house selling bread, vegetables and fresh fish.

Constantinople had no distinctly fashionable residential quarters. The houses of the very rich were often flanked by modest homes of the middle class or even the shelters of the poor. A certain amount of privacy, however, was achieved by the wealthy because their houses presented a largely blank stone wall to the street while the rooms opened out on an interior courtyard. The court invariably had a fountain and was often elaborately landscaped. Maintained by staffs of slaves and servants, the interiors of these mansions boasted a splendor of gold-plated and ivory-inlaid furniture, gilded ceilings and pillared halls. Moderately well-off citizens usually lived in two-story wooden buildings that supported balconies from which matrons and cloistered young girls could view the bustle of the street. The poor crowded in basement rooms or in the clumps of tenements spread throughout the city. As another French visitor, Odon de Deuil, wryly commented, "the rich cover the public ways with their constructions and leave the sewers and dark places to the poor and strangers. There are committed murders, robberies, and all the crimes which haunt obscurity...."

For even the poor, however, the supply of fresh water—so important in a Mediterranean climate—was plentiful. Channeled into the city through aqueducts from the surrounding hills, water was stored in many open and covered cisterns. From these it was piped to fountains at street corners and in the public squares, and was available to everyone without charge. Sewage and waste water were carried away from the houses and down into the sea through an intricate system of underground drains. The city had many public baths, open to men and women at different times, and medical and hospital care was provided by the government and the Church to those who could not afford to pay. Despite these precautions, however, disease spread quickly and always took a terrible toll.

The main street of the city, running from the landward walls in the west almost to the gates of the Imperial Palace, was called the Mesê, or Middle Street. Bordered by columned porticoes and interrupted by monumental squares containing the statues of emperors and empresses, it was the regal highway. All major imperial processions followed the Mesê. Here too were many of the fine shops of the city, piled with the products of Byzantium's luxury industries: silks and brocades, copper and goldwork, leather and glass, jewels and reliquaries. Where the street ended, close to the Imperial Palace, the perfumers had their stalls, so that, as a contemporary source had it, "the sweet perfumes may waft upward . . . and at the same time permeate the vestibule of the Imperial Palace."

In this street too could best be observed something of the variety of the city's population, estimated to have totaled some 600,000 at the time of Justinian. The inhabitants made up a thoroughly cosmopolitan group. There were natives of Cappadocia and Phrygia, close-cropped Bulgars and turbaned Persians, Jews from Palestine and Syrians from Damascus, Illyrians, Armenians and Goths. By the Ninth Century, few of the residents could boast pure Greek or Roman lineage; most had sprung from an amalgam of the many peoples the Byzantine empire comprised. The criteria for citizenship were simply the use of Greek in everyday speech and membership in the Orthodox Church.

But apart from the cosmopolitan background of its residents, the city, as a prosperous seaport and the capital of the world's largest empire, drew all manner of visitors from afar. From Britain, Spain and Gaul, from Scandinavia and Russia, from Persia, Arabia and Africa came a host of merchants, sailors, diplomats and travelers. Mingling in the streets with the more simply garbed Byzantines, these visitors, with their exotic dress—brightly colored cloaks, furs, strange headdresses—and their unfamiliar tongues, would attract considerable attention. On the streets too could be seen the many slaves, often prisoners taken in war, who performed the menial tasks in Byzantium.

Occasionally, on the main street, a court dignitary in a costume of brocaded silk would go by on horseback, or a well-to-do lady would pass, reclining in a brightly decorated carriage pulled by mules. More than likely she would be on her way to the Baths of Zeuxippus, where smart society women convened to show off their new clothes and jewelry and to exchange the latest gossip. On national holidays and religious celebrations, the whole city would turn out to watch the magnificent procession of the emperor and his court, accompanied by the patriarch and his attendants. Many in the throng of spectators could be recognized by the type of clothing they wore: philosophers usually wore gray, physicians wore blue and ascetics dressed in robes of bright scarlet with their hair confined close to their head by a net.

The life of the city was centered around three great structures or groups of buildings—the Hippodrome, the Sacred Imperial Palace, and the Church of Hagia Sophia. They represented the three main constituents of the Byzantine world: the people, the imperial authority and the religion. Appropriately, they were located close together on the central tableland and the southern and eastern slopes of the promontory on which the city stood. Here they enclosed on three sides the main public square, the Augustaeum, an open rectangular court paved with slabs of dark marble and encircled by a colonnade. Here an emperor-to-be was raised aloft on a shield and acclaimed by his nobles and the populace on his way to the coronation in Hagia Sophia. Here stood a huge bronze equestrian statue of the Emperor Justinian, clothed in what was known as Achilles' armor, wearing a plumed helmet, and carrying a globe in his left hand, signifying, as Procopius wrote, that all the earth and the sea were subject to him.

The Hippodrome, as enlarged by Constantine, could seat some 60,000 spectators; it was then 1,300 feet long and about 490 feet wide. Down the center ran the *spina*—the backbone—a low stone barrier with three cones at each end marking the turning points of the course. Along the top of the *spina* rested works of ancient art. One of these was a tall monolithic obelisk of porphyry, which came from the Temple of Karnak in Egypt. Put into position at the Hippodrome in 390 A.D., it still stands on a base with a bas-relief showing the emperor and his family in the royal box at the games.

Also still standing is the so-called obelisk of Constantine VII Porphyrogenitus. Once covered with plates of bronze decorated with bas-reliefs, it is now only a tall, thin shaft of bare masonry. A third monument which adorned the *spina* and of which something still remains is the bronze serpentine column brought from Delphi by Constantine the Great. Originally it consisted of three entwined serpents whose heads supported a golden tripod. Today only about 18 feet remains of what was probably a column of some 26 feet.

At the northeast end of the Hippodrome, which ran along one side of the square of the Augustaeum, stood the imperial box, the *kathisma*. From here the emperor and the high dignitaries of the court

(though not the empress, who had a place of her own in one of the palace churches overlooking the Hippodrome) watched the races and the public games, and presided at the execution of a criminal or at the official celebration of a victory of Byzantine arms on some remote border of the empire.

Flanking the Hippodrome to the east and also opening out onto the square of the Augustaeum lay the Sacred Imperial Palace, the residence of the emperor. It was entered through a monumental vestibule. This vestibule was known as the Brazen Entrance—the Chalkê—for its roof and doors were of gilded bronze. Its ceilings, as reconstructed by Justinian and further renovated in the Ninth Century, were covered with mosaics, some showing Justinian's great general, Belisarius, returning victoriously to Constantinople. The walls and floors were dressed with fine marbles: emerald, red and white, broken with undulating lines of blue.

Behind the Chalkê lay the vast, rambling palace itself, stretching south and southeast down the woody slopes of the promontory to the Sea of Marmara and the Bosporus. It consisted of various groups of buildings interspersed with gardens, terraces, isolated summer pavilions, churches, fountains, a private stadium, an indoor riding school, a polo ground, swimming pools and lily ponds. There were also storerooms, kitchens, stables, servants' quarters, guardrooms, dungeons.

One of the most astonishing of the buildings was the *Chrysotriclinos*, the hall of gold. This was one of the emperor's throne rooms. The throne was set in an apse; above it was an image of Christ enthroned, and before it hung a curtain of silk woven with gold and ornamented with precious stones. Elsewhere in this hall were other imperial thrones, a gold and silver banqueting table, couches, engraved plates, crowns, chandeliers, crosses and imperial vestments.

Another palace was known as the Magnaura.

This contained the famous "throne of Solomon." Reached by six steps, this royal seat was flanked by golden lions and trees of gilded bronze, their branches set with jeweled and enameled birds.

The New Palace, built in the Ninth Century with its chief hall in the form of a basilica, had a magnificent colonnade in which eight columns of verd antique alternated with eight of red onyx. The imperial bedchamber was floored with strips of marble radiating outward from a central medallion that framed a peacock in mosaic. Four eagles in mosaic stretched their wings at the foot of the four walls. The lower halves of the walls were covered with plaques of multicolored glass and shimmered like a field of flowers. Above the wainscoting and against a background of gold were mosaic portraits of members of the imperial family, their hands raised toward the brilliant green cross on the ceiling.

Between all these buildings and the sea wall at the bottom of the hill lay the imperial gardens. Here there were shaded walks and fountains; one expelled wine through a golden pineapple into a silverbound basin full of almonds and pistachios. Here ibis, peacocks and pheasants wandered among shrubs and flowers. Here stood the porphyry—or purple—chamber reserved for the birth of imperial children, from which came the title, "born in the purple" *(Porphyrogenitus)*, which was conferred on children of the ruling family. Here too was the monumental stairway leading down to the emperor's private harbor, the Boucoleon, where the royal barges and yachts lay alongside marble quays decorated with sculpture.

But not even all the manifold splendors of the palaces, none of which has endured, was exceeded by the glories of the great church of Hagia Sophia as reconstructed by Justinian. It survives, serving now as a museum, as one of the supreme artistic expressions of the Christian world. "Glory be to God, who has thought me worthy to finish this

AN ORNATE HORN, *carved of ivory, was probably used to start races or to accompany dancers in Constantinople's Hippodrome. The arena's vigorous amusements are indicated by the figures of charioteers, horsemen, jugglers and trained animals.*

work. Solomon, I have outdone thee!" So Justinian is reported to have exclaimed when he first viewed the immense majesty of the completed edifice. He celebrated its dedication in 537 with a banquet at which 6,000 sheep, 1,000 each of oxen, pigs and poultry, and 500 deer were roasted for the delectation of court and populace alike.

No expense was spared in making this church a magnificent interplay of stone, marble, light, color and space. No verbal description can do more than convey a very limited idea of it. What perhaps most strikes the viewer is the fluid nature of the architecture. This was achieved through the selection of the marble slabs which make up the floor and panel the walls. Each slab has its own pattern of veining, its own tone and shade, and yet each was cut and cut again to make it merge with its neighbor. Because of this, the stones appear as fields of alternating color, mobile strips of smoky blue or darkish green or warm red. Rows of pillars—porphyry, verd antique—form the nave and carry the small arches that support the galleries. Larger arches are surmounted by half-domes and above them hovers the great dome itself—the dome of all domes of the Byzantine world. Seen from below, it gives the impression of hovering in weightless suspense; as Procopius put it, it "seems not to rest upon solid masonry but to cover the space beneath as though suspended from heaven." This effect is emphasized by the corona of windows above its interior cornice, which makes the bases of the powerful interior ribs that support Hagia Sophia's dome seem less substantial; actually the ribs do become more delicate as they soar upward toward the crown of the dome.

Light is one of the essential elements contributing to the overall effect of the church. Pouring down from the corona of windows in the dome, flooding in from lunettes in the half-domes, it steeps the central nave in radiance. At night the Byzantines continued this play of light by lamp and candle. Thousands of lamps hung by long, twisted chains of beaten brass from the dome and the ceilings, casting their glow on the shimmering gold mosaic of vaults and arches, playing gently over the lambent surfaces of the colored marble, turning the whole church into a brilliant beacon of light. A contemporary poet, Paul the Silentiary, describes the splendor of the church at night in a long poem which he wrote for its dedication:

"Thus through the spaces of the great church come rays of light, expelling clouds of care, and filling the mind with joy. The sacred light cheers all; even the sailor guiding his bark on the waves, leaving behind him the unfriendly billows of the raging Pontus, and winding a sinuous course amidst creeks and rocks, with heart fearful at the dangers of his nightly wanderings—perhaps he has left the Aegean and guides his ship against adverse currents in the Hellespont, awaiting with taut forestay the onslaught of a storm from Africa—does not guide his laden vessel by the light of Cynosure, or the circling Bear, but by the divine light of the church itself. Yet not only does it guide the merchant at night, like the rays of Pharos on the coast of Africa, but it also shows the way to the living God."

Hagia Sophia was the crowning glory of the city which was the capital, and the heart, of the Byzantine world, that "queen of cities." Restless compound of Greece and Rome, of Europe and Asia, metropolis of commerce and fountainhead of culture, it drew to itself Jew and Moslem, Russian and Italian, Spaniard and Egyptian. Its architecture influenced the ecclesiastical architecture of other historic cities—Ravenna, Venice, Kiev, Moscow. Above all, it was the center from which Byzantine history unfolded—that record of splendor and corruption, sophistication and imagery, order and anarchy, of great victories and petty vanities—a history which deeply affected the history of the civilized world.

THE TOWER OF GALATA, *Constantinople's highest observation point, overlooks the ship-thronged Golden Horn and a skyline dominated by Hagia Sophia's dome.*

A CAPITAL OBSERVED

For 11 centuries Byzantium's capital was a showpiece of Roman city planning and Christian piety, a city where squads of soldiers paraded through classical forums chanting "Christ the Conqueror" and imperial senators worshiped in gilded basilicas. Visitors to the city found masses of classical statuary adorning public buildings and reported seeing angels hovering over Hagia Sophia's altars. Though Byzantium's capital had its share of poverty, filth and injustice, for the most part Constantinople was a well-run metropolis with free hospitals, street lighting and fire brigades. But today only scattered glimpses remain of its civic achievements, now partly buried beneath the streets of modern Turkish Istanbul. In this essay, following a map reconstructing the Byzantine city, the British artist Paul Hogarth has sketched impressions of Constantinople in its glory.

41

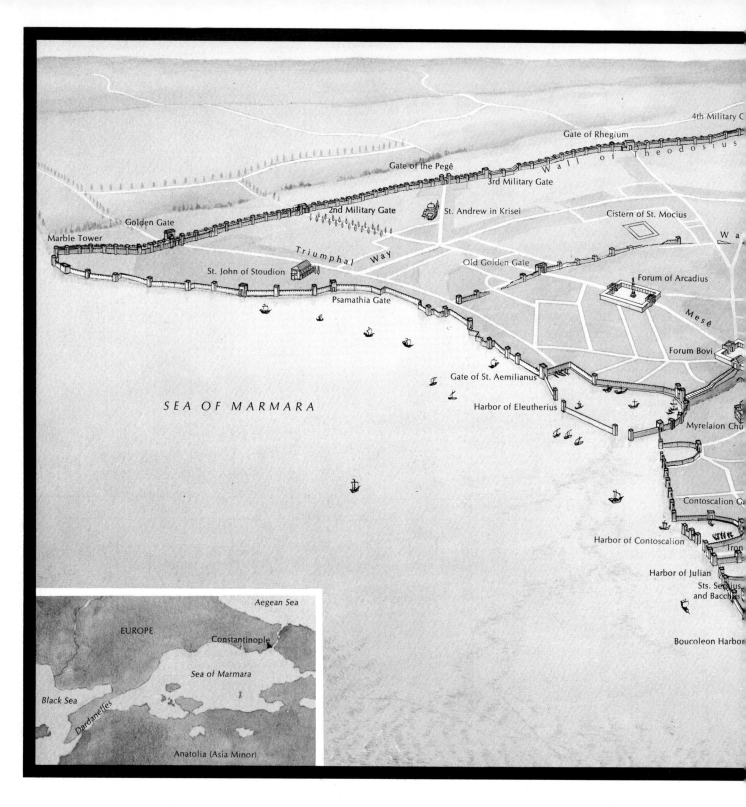

Within the map:

4th Military G
Gate of Rhegium
Gate of the Pegê
Wall of Theodosius
3rd Military Gate
2nd Military Gate
St. Andrew in Krisei
Cistern of St. Mocius
W a
Golden Gate
Marble Tower
Triumphal Way
St. John of Stoudion
Old Golden Gate
Forum of Arcadius
Psamathia Gate
Mese
Forum Bovi
Gate of St. Aemilianus
SEA OF MARMARA
Harbor of Eleutherius
Myrelaion Chu
Contoscalion G
Harbor of Contoscalion
Iron
Harbor of Julian
Sts. Sergius
and Bacch
Boucoleon Harbor

Inset map:

Aegean Sea
EUROPE
Constantinople
Sea of Marmara
Black Sea
Dardanelles
Anatolia (Asia Minor)

A RICH AND HOLY FORTRESS

"She is the glory of the Greeks, rich in repute, and even richer in reality," declared a French pilgrim who visited Constantinople in 1147. As the map above shows, the city's geography contributed generously to Constantinople's legendary richness. Sprawling across an easily defended wedge of hilly ground at the mouth of the Bosporus (see inset map), Constantinople prospered by controlling the major caravan routes from China, India and Persia, and the narrow straits that funneled into its walled harbors all the seaborne traffic passing between the Mediterranean and the Black Sea.

As the imperial capital and a center of commerce, Constantinople

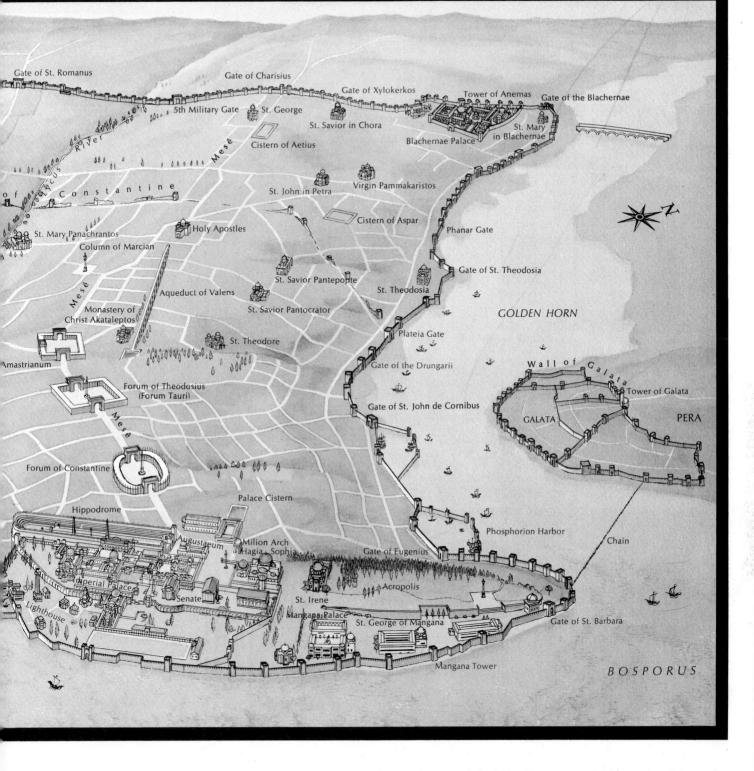

Gate of St. Romanus

Gate of Charisius

Gate of Xylokerkos

Tower of Anemas

Gate of the Blachernae

5th Military Gate

St. George

St. Savior in Chora

Blachernae Palace

St. Mary
in Blachernae

Cistern of Aetius

River

Mese

of Constantine

St. John in Petra

Virgin Pammakaristos

Phanar Gate

St. Mary Panachrantos

Holy Apostles

Cistern of Aspar

Gate of St. Theodosia

Column of Marcian

St. Theodosia

Mese

St. Savior Pantepopte

St. Theodosia

Aqueduct of Valens

GOLDEN HORN

Monastery of
Christ Akataleptos

St. Savior Pantocrator

Plateia Gate

St. Theodore

Wall of Galata

Amastrianum

Gate of the Drungarii

Tower of Galata

Forum of Theodosius
(Forum Tauri)

Gate of St. John de Cornibus

GALATA

PERA

Mese

Forum of Constantine

Phosphorion Harbor

Chain

Palace Cistern

Hippodrome

Augustaeum

Milion Arch
Hagia Sophia

Gate of Eugenius

Acropolis

Imperial Palace

Senate

St. Irene

Gate of St. Barbara

Lighthouse

Mangana Palace

St. George of Mangana

Mangana Tower

BOSPORUS

attracted a polyglot population of Greeks, Bulgars, Khazars, Turks, Armenians, Jews, Russians and Italians. With nearly a million inhabitants at its peak the city rivaled classical Rome in size, and Rome's civic structures remained for centuries the models that inspired Constantinople's architects and engineers. Public baths, Senate buildings, forums, basilicas and commemorative columns lined the city's broad avenues, which converged on a downtown center at the Hippodrome, Hagia Sophia and the Imperial Palace. As in Rome, aqueducts insured the populace of clean water at all times, and underground sewers carried off the city's wastes. Since one of Rome's 14

districts lay across the Tiber River, one of Constantinople's 14 districts was placed across the Golden Horn in Pera, where Genoese merchants later made their homes.

Built to withstand barbarian hordes and Moslem armies, Constantinople was the strongest outpost of Christianity in the East. Thirteen miles of walls and 50 fortified gates made the city a self-contained fortress, with enormous grain reserves and cisterns to sustain its inhabitants during sieges. A line of triple walls, watchtowers and a moat guarded the city's landward side, while walled harbors and a chain across the Golden Horn protected ships from attacks by sea.

THE GOLDEN GATE *(left)*, reserved for state processions, was Constantinople's most dramatic landward entrance. Newly crowned emperors and victorious generals were acclaimed as they passed under its triumphal archways. Inside the wall hymn-singing citizens thronged beneath olive and cypress trees to watch the army escort wagons of treasure and columns of prisoners along the flower-strewn Mesê, the city's commercial boulevard, to the Hippodrome. There captives were sometimes startled by offers of land and citizenship—rather than execution—but only if they renounced their pagan deities.

CONSTANTINE'S FORUM *(below)*, dominated by a shaft of porphyry topped with a gold cross, was the largest of the city's six public forums. Here emperors celebrated their triumphs with victory hymns and waving banners; here lawyers and merchants met to talk over business, fortunetellers harangued superstitious crowds, aristocratic women arrived in sedan chairs to gossip in the shade of double-tiered arcades. Other forums were centers of commerce. The Atropoleum had a bread market; the Forum of Theodosius served for pig slaughtering; and flocks of sheep often thronged the Strategion.

A NOISY MAZE OF TENEMENTS *(below)*, often jammed with caravan traffic, surrounded Constantinople's forums. Though building codes demanded 12-foot-wide streets, true city planning was a luxury not wasted on the poor. Refuse-heaped alleys meandered past houses, stables, taverns and warehouses, and plagues took a heavy toll. But few starved or went homeless. As many as 80,-000 loaves of bread were distributed daily to the poor, and monasteries always provided a haven for the hard-pressed.

OPEN-AIR BAZAARS, shaded by canopies (*above*), displayed everything from figs to icons. Commerce was strictly regulated by city officials: linen drapers could not sell silks, fishermen had to register their catch and goldsmiths were fined for hoarding. Yet the city's planned economy prospered. "Wealth like that of Constantinople," wrote the widely traveled Benjamin of Tudela, "is not to be found in the whole world."

SHOEMAKERS AND LEATHERWORKERS, like most of Constantinople's craftsmen, could set up shops only in streets and arcades assigned by the city prefect. Laws regulating trade encouraged specialized skills; leatherworkers, for example, were forbidden to tan hides. Guilds set standards, specified materials, and punished the careless. As a result, the city's craftsmen produced goods finer than most Western visitors had ever seen.

THE HIPPODROME:
A VAST ARENA
FOR PUBLIC SPECTACLES

Constantinople's Hippodrome, almost in the shadow of the dome of Hagia Sophia *(glimpsed at far right),* provided the city's Christian populace with virtually all the spectacle and violence of Rome's Circus Maximus, on which it was closely modeled. Though the 1,300-foot-long Hippodrome was originally designed for chariot races, changing fashions put its arena to many uses—mock hunts, acrobatics, mystery plays. After the 12th Century, spectators even witnessed the unusual sight, pictured here, of Western jousts in a Roman-style stadium studded with classical monuments and decorative columns.

At such events the emperor, guarded by soldiers, presided above the arena in his *kathisma,* or royal box. Sometimes his presence could turn the Hippodrome into an enormous civic forum where the people might protest oppressive taxes; at other times the spectators could witness the execution of corrupt officials. But in times of upheaval this same populace—which the Emperor Isaac Angelus compared to the violent and unpredictable Calydonian boar—took over the Hippodrome as its own. Here the Emperor Andronicus I was tortured and executed in 1185, and here during the Nika rebellion in 532 the army trapped and massacred 30,000 rioting citizens who had tried to elect a new emperor.

ST. THEODORE TYRO, with its domed chapels of marble and brick, drew worshipers from a district near the Aqueduct of Valens, and its congregation shared a typically Byzantine fascination with theological issues. After Bishop Gregory of Nyssa visited the city he remarked wryly: "People swarm everywhere talking of incomprehensible matters. When I ask how many coppers I must pay, they reply with minute distinctions on the Born and the Unborn. I ask the servant if my bath is ready, and he replies that the Son was created from Nothing."

ST. MARY PANACHRANTOS grew haphazardly over the centuries from a small chapel into an irregular cluster of separate churches and galleries, and was ultimately crowned with Turkish cupolas. Its architects lavished their skills on dramatic interior spaces and mosaics; outside decorations were left to imaginative masons, who spaced out valuable building stone with friezes and rosettes of brick in colored mortar.

HAGIA SOPHIA loomed high over Constantinople's other churches, and to the faithful its immense cascade of domes symbolized Christianity's all-embracing heavens. Over 100 feet across and 180 feet high, the Great Church's vaulted interior long surpassed in size all the churches of Europe, and "from earth soaring upward to the blue, reached even to the choirs of the stars." Built by Justinian in 537, Hagia Sophia remained the nerve center that ruled the Orthodox Christian world for nine centuries. Although its patriarchs were appointed by the emperor, they often wielded great influence of their own; the most zealous excommunicated whole communities of heretics. Missionaries from the Great Church spread Byzantine culture throughout Eastern Europe and Russia, until the Turks conquered the city in 1453 and converted the church into a mosque.

ST. SAVIOR IN CHORA, built by Justinian I, stood originally in the meadows outside the city, but Constantinople's rapid growth soon surrounded it with houses and shops. Gradually it fell into decay. But when the Comnenus dynasty moved to the nearby Blachernae Palace in the mid-12th Century, St. Savior was restored and lavishly decorated. About 150 years later the interior was embellished with a blaze of mosaics and frescoes. But by then the emperors were too poor to spend money on churches and the work was paid for by a private patron.

THE BOUCOLEON PALACE *(below)* overlooked the imperial yacht basin and a wharf decorated with statues of lions and other animals. From this palace, which was one of seven royal residences, stretched a labyrinth of buildings and gardens that comprised the Imperial Palace complex. Blazing mosaics and marbles made it a scene of unmatched beauty. Landscaped with pavilions, fountains and fishponds, the palace had an air of park-like tranquility. But it was also a hive of practical activity: 20,000 citizens worked within its walls as civil servants, entertainers, guards, courtiers and priests. And in the palace workshops, artisans manufactured fine weapons, dyes, and high-grade silks—state monopolies whose profits supported many imperial bureaucrats.

THE PALACE OF CONSTANTINE PORPHYROGENITUS *(right)* was incorporated into an angle of the city's walls, in the Blachernae palace district that the Byzantine court occupied after the 12th Century. As the empire declined, the court continued to embellish itself with a rich array of ceremonies to underscore the Emperor's divinity. Processions marched back and forth in a cloud of incense between palaces and churches; more than 30 religious ceremonies every month demanded the Emperor's participation. Meals in the palace imitated the Last Supper, and clumsy servants could be decapitated for dropping a plate. As ruler of the New Jerusalem, the Emperor owned symbolic costumes for every occasion—at Easter, for example, he commemorated Christ's resurrection by wearing a burial shroud and whitening his face to resemble a corpse.

3
CHRONICLE
OF AN EMPIRE

During the 1,123 years of its existence—from 330 to 1453 A.D.—Byzantium's boundaries were continually in a state of flux. In the age of Justinian, in the Sixth Century, they extended from Spain in the west to the plains of Mesopotamia in the east, and from the Black Sea and the Danube in the north to the coastal fringe of Mediterranean Africa in the south. During the last decades of the Palaeologus dynasty, Byzantium's final period, the empire's borders had shrunk until they embraced only the city itself and parts of southern Greece.

Actually, it is impossible to specify any one year as the birth date of Byzantium. Constantine's designation of the city as his capital did not at once inaugurate a Byzantine empire as distinct from the Roman. No doubt the seeds of transformation were present in Constantine's conversion to Christianity and in his founding of a new capital on the Bosporus; and no doubt Constantine himself possessed an almost mystical apprehension of the immense change he was initiating. But in other respects the first phase of Byzantine history—from 330 to the death of Anastasius I in 518—was little more than an attempt to strengthen and defend the old Roman Empire against the forces that threatened its existence.

Christianity, meanwhile, was spreading its influence as the state suppressed paganism with increasing harshness. For a brief period, however, under Emperor Julian (361-363), an attempt was made to turn back the sundial and restore the gods of antiquity. Julian, though brought up as a Christian, was exposed from early youth to the teachings of the ancient Greeks, and became a fervent adherent of the ancient Hellenistic rites (thus earning an immortal sobriquet, "the Apostate"). On becoming emperor he strengthened paganism by reorganizing its priesthood and by taking part personally in its services, kindling the altar fire, wielding the knife and inspecting the entrails of the slaughtered birds for omens of the future. At the same time he attempted to weaken Christianity by removing Christians from military and civil posts and forbidding them to teach the works of Homer, Hesiod and the other great pagan writers. When he closed churches, violence broke out and anarchy threatened. With his death his successors reversed his policies until in the reign of Theodosius the Great (379-395)

PATRON OF ARMIES, *a soldierly St. George adorns a 12th Century Byzantine plaque. The virtues of such "warrior saints," sanctity and valor, were greatly admired by a holy empire constantly at war with its neighbors.*

SUEV

Córde

Septum

Christianity was designated as the state religion.

During this opening period between the Fourth and the early Sixth Centuries, the eastern half of the empire largely escaped the disasters that overtook the western half as the barbarian invaders swept into Italy and other Roman possessions in the West. True, in the second half of the Fourth Century the appearance of the Huns in Eastern Europe drove the Germanic tribes that had settled there across the borders of Byzantium. But after they defeated Byzantine forces at Adrianople in 378, the Germanic tribes were mollified by the great Theodosius, who offered them full autonomy, grants of land and service at high pay in the imperial forces. In the West, on the other hand, the barbarian onslaught brought about the downfall of the empire. By the early part of the Sixth Century, Italy was in the hands of the Ostrogoths, Gaul had been seized by the Franks, the Visigoths held Spain and the Vandals had conquered North Africa. The West had entered into that period of turmoil and darkness in which its independent destiny was to be forged.

Spared the more devastating consequences of the barbarian migrations which had inundated the West, Byzantium had been able to preserve intact its heritage of Greco-Roman civilization and culture. At the same time it was during this period that the basic theological dogma of Orthodox Christianity had been hammered out and proclaimed at the great councils of the Church, particularly at the Council of Chalcedon in 451. The stage was now set for the full emergence of the civilization implicit in Constantine the Great's acceptance of Christ as "Ruler and Master of the Universe."

Byzantium's emergence was in part accomplished in the period that stretches from the opening of the reign of the Emperor Justin I in 518 and closes with the death of the Emperor Phocas in 610. Straddling the center of this period—the years from 527 to 565—towers the great figure of the last of the great Roman emperors, Justinian I. It was during his reign that major aspects of the Byzantine world, as distinct from the Roman world, began to assume their definitive form.

Mosaic portraits of Justinian reveal a man who did not look the part of emperor. He was of average height and build, with dark hair and ruddy complexion; his bland face was clean shaven and he seems to have worn a habitual faint smile. But this inconspicuous figure of a man was gifted with intelligence and talents such as few rulers possessed; and he played his imperial role up the hilt—with affability, arrogance and enormous vigor.

Justinian was about 45 years old when he assumed the purple. He was born of a family of Balkan peasants lately come up in the world. His unlettered uncle Justin, who had arrived in the capital with a bag of bread on his back, had fought his way to the throne through the ranks of the army. Justin educated Justinian, and the younger man then earned the throne in his own right by brilliant service as his uncle's chief aide. As emperor he thrived on a strict and taxing regimen. He ate little and fasted often; he arose early and worked late on affairs of state. After a full day of intense concentration, he usually studied late into the night to enlarge his considerable knowledge of law, theology, music and architecture. Yet in spite of his crowded schedule, Justinian was—as his unfriendly biographer Procopius admitted—"the most accessible person in the world. For even men of low estate and altogether obscure had complete freedom not only to come before him but to converse with him."

Justinian's wife, Theodora, was an equally remarkable person. She was an actress and a courtesan, daughter of a bear-keeper at the Hippodrome. According to Procopius, before her marriage she had so great a reputation for debauchery that people avoided her in the streets. But she possessed other qualities, including intelligence, compassion,

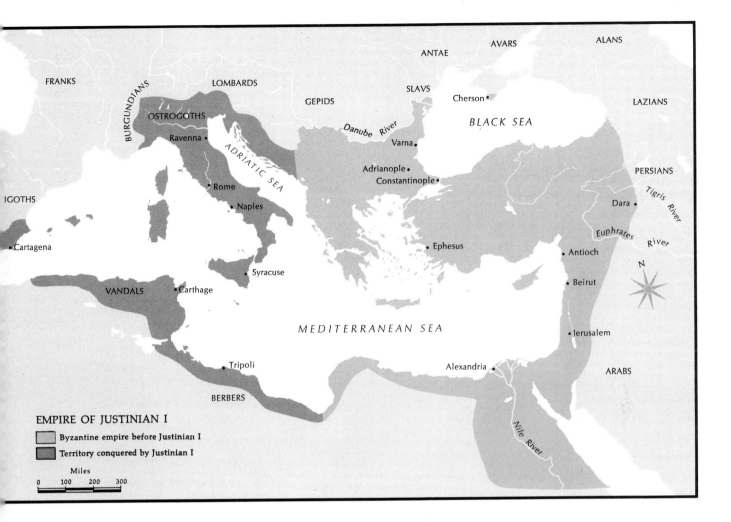

EMPIRE OF JUSTINIAN I

▨ Byzantine empire before Justinian I

▨ Territory conquered by Justinian I

Miles
0   100   200   300

and courage, as she was to demonstrate. In any case, Justinian fell violently in love with her. At first she was only his mistress, for a man of senatorial rank was barred by law from marrying an actress. But Justinian succeeded in having the law changed and Theodora became his wife and empress.

It was Theodora who was said to have prevented Justinian from flight during the Nika riots in 532. "I hold that now if ever flight is inexpedient, even if it brings safety," she said. "When a man has once been born into the light, it is inevitable that he should also meet death. But for an emperor to become a fugitive is a thing not to be endured. . . . If you wish to flee to safety, Emperor, it can easily be done . . . there is the sea; here are the ships. But as for me, I hold with the old saying that royalty makes a fine winding-sheet."

Theodora's autocratic behavior also had less attractive aspects. Tales were told of secret private dungeons in her palace into which people she dis-

approved of disappeared forever. More congenial is the story of how she sheltered a deposed patriarch in her own apartments for 12 years without anyone knowing of it. Ruthless in her own cause, and capable of using any means to get her way, she nevertheless equipped Constantinople with hospitals for the poor, and converted an old palace on the bank of the Bosporus into a home for destitute women.

Justinian was obsessed by the dream of restoring the original Roman Empire in all its integrity. "We have good hope," he wrote in an official edict, "that God will allow us to reconquer the lands of the old Roman Empire which have been lost through indolence." Prudence should have led him to concentrate on consolidating his eastern borders, where the pressures of a restored Persian empire had grown since the beginning of the Sixth Century. Instead he bought off the Persians by agreeing to pay the Persian king a large annual tribute and threw all his forces, under the brilliant generalship first of Beli-sarius and then of Narses, into an effort to recap-ture the western and African provinces lost to the Germanic tribes.

In 533 Belisarius broke the control of the Van-dals in North Africa. Two years after this the By-zantines occupied Sicily, and in 536 Belisarius entered Rome. By the time of Justinian's death, the Ostrogoths had been conquered in Italy, other is-lands in the western Mediterranean—Corsica, Sar-dinia and the Balearics—had been regained and By-zantine forces had penetrated into southeast Spain. The larger part of Spain remained in Visigothic control, and the province of Gaul was never recap-tured. Even so, before he died Justinian may well have thought that the dream of restoring the an-cient unity of the empire was on the verge of reali-zation. Indeed, for the last time, the *imperium ro-manum*, as the Byzantine empire was still called, did include almost the entire Mediterranean world.

Justinian set out to restore the Roman Empire internally as well as geographically. To reform the administration he abolished the sale of offices and centralized the bureaucracy. His widespread build-ing program included new fortifications in Europe and in Asia. Justinian's greatest and most lasting monument to Byzantine society—indeed, to West-ern society—was his recodification of Roman law. At his instigation a legal commission, under the direction of Tribonian, produced a series of books, known as the *Corpus* of Justinian, in which an attempt was made to summarize and bring up to date the many components of the Roman legal sys-tem. This great work, preserving the heritage of Roman law, formed the basis of the Byzantine le-gal system. When it was received in the West in the 11th Century it helped shape the development of Latin legal and political thought, and thus passed into the stream of world history.

In his attitude toward the Church, Justinian retained the tradition of the pagan emperors of Rome. As the pagan emperors had been not only masters of the government but also chief arbiters in the religious affairs of the empire, Justinian—and many of his predecessors and successors on the Byzantine throne—sought to dominate both Church and state. His interest in the Church, his support of missionary work, his promotion of monasticism, and his own concern for theology were all genuine. But for him the state, as a sacred instrument for forging a Christian Roman empire, was what really counted.

This meant in practical terms that for Justinian religious unity and state unity were one and the same thing. Although Christianity had been de-clared the state religion, remnants of paganism had lingered on. Seeking to eradicate them, Justinian closed down the university at Athens, paganism's last stronghold. At the same time, his desire to re-habilitate the empire in the West led him to seek the support of its one stable element, the papacy.

This in its turn meant aggravation of an already serious domestic-religious controversy centering around the doctrine of Monophysitism, which ex-alted Christ's divinity at the expense of His hu-manity—a doctrine condemned under papal pres-sure by the Council of Chalcedon in 451. In the Byzantine provinces of Egypt and Syria, where Monophysitism was strong, Justinian, conscious of the importance of these provinces to his empire and influenced by Theodora, who had Monophysite leanings, first tried to conciliate the heretics. But pressure from the pope soon forced him into a policy of vacillation—with concessions made now to the pope, now to the Monophysites. Such con-cessions as Justinian and his immediate succes-sors granted failed to placate the Monophysites, however, and their antagonism toward Constanti-nople mounted. Approximately a century later, the Egyptians and the Syrians were to greet first the

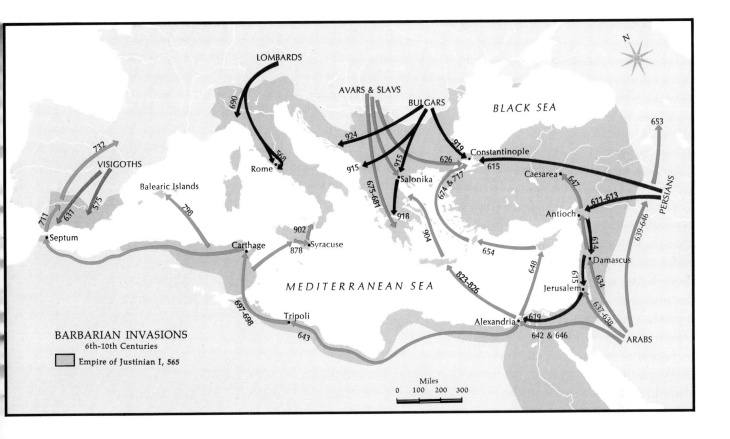

LOMBARDS

AVARS & SLAVS

BULGARS

BLACK SEA

VISIGOTHS

Balearic Islands

Rome

Septum

Carthage

Syracuse

Constantinople

Caesarea

Antioch

Salonika

PERSIANS

Damascus

MEDITERRANEAN SEA

Jerusalem

Tripoli

Alexandria

ARABS

BARBARIAN INVASIONS
6th-10th Centuries

Empire of Justinian I, 565

Miles
0 100 200 300

Persian conquerors and then the forces of Islam as liberators from the religious and political oppression of Byzantium.

In the end Justinian's dream of restoring the Roman Empire remained only a dream. A few years after his death in 565 the work of this last Roman Emperor—the Emperor "who never sleeps"—began to fall apart. In 568 the Lombards invaded Italy. By the early Seventh Century, lands that Justinian had regained in Spain were again in Visigothic hands; from the north had come invasions from the Avars, and the Persians had conquered parts of Syria, Palestine and Egypt. The empire itself was on the verge of anarchy and bankruptcy.

Justinian's religious policy may have been dictated by reasons of state; nevertheless what it confirmed was the triumph of the doctrine of the Incarnate Word over the pagan cults of Rome. And in the great church of Hagia Sophia as finally built by Justinian, in other contemporary churches in Constantinople, Jerusalem, Ravenna and elsewhere, in the intensity and spirituality of so much monas-

tic literature produced during his reign; in all this may be seen the first flowering of Byzantine genius, transcending the ephemeral glory of Justinian's territorial conquests.

The disintegration which beset the empire in the years after Justinian was temporarily halted by the Emperor Heraclius (610-641). Rallying his people and draining the churches and the provinces for funds, he took the offensive against the invaders. The Avars were bought off with a considerable sum of money and with distinguished hostages from the Byzantine court. The Persians were defeated in a series of campaigns, and Egypt, Syria and Palestine were returned to Byzantine rule. The True Cross, which the Persians had removed from Jerusalem, was triumphantly restored to the Holy Land. Heraclius also began the organization of the empire into a series of military provinces, or themes, a system which was to remain the basis of government for the next five centuries.

Heraclius' successes were only a respite, however, for mounted tribesmen from central Arabia

—the followers of the Prophet Mohammed—were riding out of the desert in search of conquest. Within 10 years after the Prophet's death in 632, these Moslem warriors had poured unchecked through Palestine, Syria, Egypt and Persia. When Heraclius died in 641 the empire had lost its most southeasterly possessions forever. By the end of the Heraclian dynasty in 711, Byzantium was reduced to the Anatolian peninsula and the Balkan coast, southern Italy and the island of Sicily. And at the end of the Seventh Century another enemy, the Bulgars, appeared in the Balkans.

In 717 Constantinople was besieged by the Moslems for the second time, and for the second time successfully defended. The first time, during a series of attacks between 673 and 677, the city was saved by the Byzantine fleet. The second time it was a powerful general of some of the troops in Anatolia who came to the rescue. Crowned as Leo III (717-741) and founder of the new Syrian dynasty, he and his son Constantine V (741-775) pushed the Moslems back to the southern fringe of Anatolia, continued the reorganization of the provinces begun under Heraclius, and thus completed the consolidation of Byzantium as a comparatively small state geared for defense against the enemies which surrounded it.

Both spiritually and territorially the worldwide Roman Empire had now been finally transformed into that of Byzantium. Having lost most of its conquests in the West and in the Middle East, Byzantium had become predominantly Greek in speech and civilization, as the Latin element in the eastern part of the empire faded. But even in lands that had been shorn from the eastern empire, Byzantium's influence in thought and culture lingered, penetrating even to territories that had never been under Byzantine rule.

The breach between Byzantium and the West was widened by a long and bitter family struggle that ultimately destroyed the Syrian dynasty. The lurid drama began in 780, when the 10-year-old Constantine VI inherited the throne. Acting as regent was his mother, the widowed Empress Irene, a woman whose dazzling beauty was equaled only by her cruelty and ambition. For years Irene easily controlled her amiable imperial offspring. But as Constantine reached maturity, he welcomed a plan that promised to free him from his mother's clutches: marriage to a daughter of the powerful Frankish king Charlemagne, whose realm had troublesome borders with Byzantium.

Eventually, the promising plan was thwarted by Irene. The disappointed Constantine, emboldened by army support, rose up and banished his mother from the palace. Irene, however, was not to be denied. After seven years of tireless conspiracy, she succeeded in having Constantine imprisoned and blinded. Thus in 797 Irene finally took the throne to rule in her own name.

Irene's triumph produced an even more sensational development in Rome. Pope Leo III saw in Constantine's fall a glowing opportunity to elevate papal prestige. Adjudging the throne to be vacant —i.e., lacking a male occupant—the Pope in 800 boldly bestowed upon Charlemagne the title and crown of emperor. To all good Byzantines, this coronation was a criminal arrogation of power, if not a sin against the sacred state; it aggravated relations between the Eastern Church and the papacy.

The East and the West drifted apart. Irene's days of glory quickly ran out. In 802 she was overthrown by a palace revolution and exiled to the island of Lesbos. There she spent her last few months in miserable isolation. To the very end, the fierce old Empress was kept under close guard to prevent her from fomenting still another revolution.

The climax of the Byzantine achievement, or the greater part of it—the years from 867 to 1056—

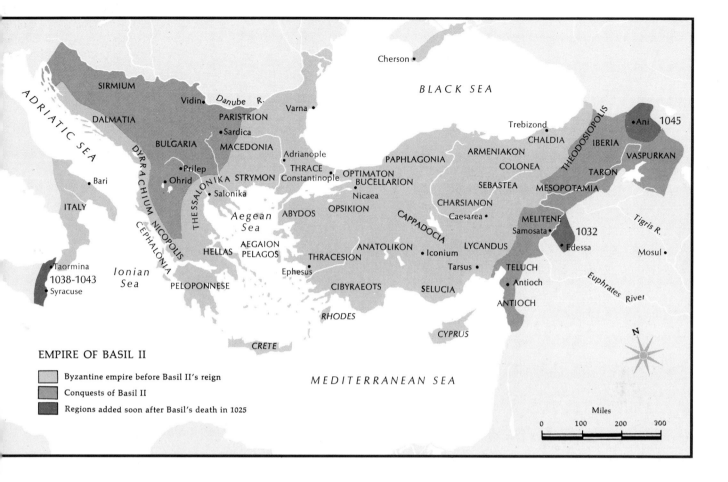

EMPIRE OF BASIL II

Byzantine empire before Basil II's reign

Conquests of Basil II

Regions added soon after Basil's death in 1025

came under the great Macedonian dynasty. This house included among its members emperors as distinguished as its founder, Basil I (867-886), whose military triumphs initiated the new era—notably Leo VI, called the Wise (886-912); Constantine VII Porphyrogenitus (913-959), a patron of the arts who compiled manuals on court ceremony and diplomacy; and Basil II Bulgaroctonus (the Bulgar-slayer, 976-1025), the austere soldier and statesman who, as his name indicates, triumphed over the Bulgars and reduced practically the whole Balkan peninsula to imperial rule.

It was a period of external expansion and internal prosperity. All the world's wealth seemed to pour through the trade routes of the Levant, overland from India and beyond, or down the great Russian rivers and the Black Sea into Constantinople, there to furnish the queen of cities with even greater splendor. The menacing forces of Islam were pushed back into the southern region of Syr-

ia as the great cities of Antioch and Aleppo were reconquered. The seizure of Crete in 961 and Cyprus in 965 marked the revival of Byzantine naval power in the eastern Mediterranean. The Slavic world of Russia was drawn into the Byzantine cultural orbit through trade and religious penetration. In 957 the Grand Princess Olga, serving as regent of the newly founded Russian state, came to Constantinople and was baptized. Her grandson, Prince Vladimir of Kiev, after assisting Basil II in crushing a rebellion, was given Basil's sister, Anna, in marriage, and converted himself and his people to Christianity.

Basil II reigned for nearly half a century as the Byzantine emperor. His speech was plain, his manner abrupt and direct. By the sophisticated standards of the civil aristocracy, he was coarse and unpolished. As the 11th Century chronicler and philosopher, Michael Psellus, remarked, he adopted an almost ascetic simplicity in his efforts to keep control over the diverse affairs of state. "He even went so far as to scorn bodily ornaments. His neck was unadorned by collars, his head by diadems. He refused to make himself conspicuous in purple-colored cloaks and he put away superfluous rings, even clothes of different colors. On the other hand, he took great pains to ensure that the various departments of the government should be centered on himself, and that they should work, without friction." From his people he required not love, but obedience.

In the East, Basil's chief adversary was the Egyptian dynasty of the Fatimids. In 994, the Fatimids defeated the Byzantine armies on the Orontes, and they followed this up by besieging Aleppo and threatening Antioch itself. Basil in person led the campaign to recover the situation. Unlike many other emperors, when it was necessary he stayed in the field throughout the winter months, steeling himself against the cold as in summer he disciplined himself against thirst. However, he was well versed in tactics and understood the combat duties of individual officers. He was thus a formidable opponent. In his Eastern campaigns he had by 999 restored the status quo in Syria, and during the rest of his reign there were no further serious threats from the Eastern Arabs.

This left Basil free to concentrate on his enemies in the West. These were the Bulgarians, who now under King Samuel, after revolting against Constantinople, had conquered all of Macedonia except Salonika, the Bulgarian territory between the Danube and the Balkan range; Thessaly; Epirus; and part of Albania. In 1001 Basil opened his counteroffensive against the Bulgars. Once again leading his armies, in four years of campaigning he reduced Samuel's territory to about half its original size. Samuel's final defeat came in 1014 at a battle in the Struma region of northern Greece. Samuel himself escaped, but Basil is said to have taken some 14,-000 prisoners. These he first blinded and then sent back to Samuel in batches of a hundred, each group led by a one-eyed man. When Samuel beheld this sightless cavalcade of his defeated soldiers, he fell senseless, and died two days later.

Basil, "slayer of the Bulgars," as he was thereafter called, had once again raised the Byzantine empire into a great power whose territories extended from the eastern reaches of the Black Sea to the Adriatic in the west, from the Danube in the north to the Euphrates in the south. He celebrated his triumph by a ceremonial march through Greece as far as Athens, where he held a service of solemn thanksgiving in the Parthenon, which had been converted into a Christian church dedicated to the Mother of God.

Yet in spite of this resurgence of Byzantine power there were signs of trouble impending. In the West, Norman adventurers were penetrating Byzantine possessions in southern Italy. The rift between the Churches of Rome and Constantinople was deepening and in 1054 the two Churches excommunicated each other. The Italian maritime republics, growing in strength, were anxious to expand their commerce. Crusader fervor was rising in the West, directed against the Infidel in the East—but eventually to covet Byzantium itself. In the north, the steppe tribes, Patzinaks and Uzes, were pouring over the long Danube frontier. At home, the structure of Byzantine society was being weakened by the growing independence and greed of a privileged landed aristocracy at the expense of small peasant proprietors and soldiers who had been granted farms in return for part-time military service. Finally, over the eastern borders lay the deepening shadow of the Seljuk Turks.

Although under the Macedonians Byzantine glory had risen to new heights, by the time the last member of the house came to the throne the tide of Byzantine history had turned—for the last time.

AS EMPEROR *(and thus as God's representative in earthly affairs), Basil sits on his throne dispensing a stern justice.*

BASIL THE MAGNIFICENT

History has few more beguiling tales than that of a self-made man who rises from obscurity to grasp an empire, enlarge its realm and polish it bright with new glories. Such an emperor was Byzantium's Basil I, who was born in the Ninth Century on a barren, rocky farm near Adrianople, in the imperial district of Macedonia. Basil spent his childhood in Bulgarian captivity, then as a young man ventured to Constantinople, where by prodigious feats of valor on hunting field, in banquet hall and in parlor (plus occasional discreet sallies in assassination) he reached the throne—and, surprisingly, turned out to be a wonderfully wise and able monarch. Many ancient chronicles tell his story, none more revealingly than the one compiled by John Scylitzes, a Byzantine official of the 11th Century. One version of Scylitzes' account was illustrated during the 14th Century by hundreds of miniatures painted by pious monks in Sicily. It now rests in Spain's National Library in Madrid, offering a rare—and sometimes wryly amusing—insight into the personalities and politics of Byzantine empiresmanship.

Baby Basil was taken by his family to the wheatfields where they worked, and placed in a bower. When the hot sun slanted in, an eagle, the imperial symbol, came to shade him. His mother tried to drive it off—until she sensed a divine sign. The small Greek labels identify characters; the larger script is Scylitzes' running account.

A portent of young Basil's future greatness came to his mother in a dream. A tall, slim cypress with trunk and leaves of gold seemed to grow from the foot of her bed; standing in it was her son. She related her vision to a wise woman, who told her that the dream clearly meant a golden destiny for Basil as Emperor of Byzantium.

Young Basil and his family, taken captive by invading Bulgarians along with thousands of other Macedonians, were released some years later by the Bulgarian King Omurtag. As the prisoners marched out of captivity (above) on their way back to their farms, Omurtag noticed the boy "smiling graciously and romping around" and reached out to grab him. Basil, unafraid, jumped up on the King's lap (right). While a nearby official protested, Omurtag kissed Basil and gave him a big apple—which was interpreted as yet another symbol of future empire.

Tired of farming, Basil left the homestead to his brothers and set out for Constantinople. He entered town at dusk of a Sunday evening and sat down to rest on the steps of the monastery of St. Diomedes. In the first of two successive scenes at right, the Saint himself appears inside the monastery and bids the Superior welcome the young man who will be emperor one day. In the second scene the monk takes the adventurer in. He later recommended Basil to a friend of Emperor Michael III, Theophilitzes, who engaged him as master of his stables.

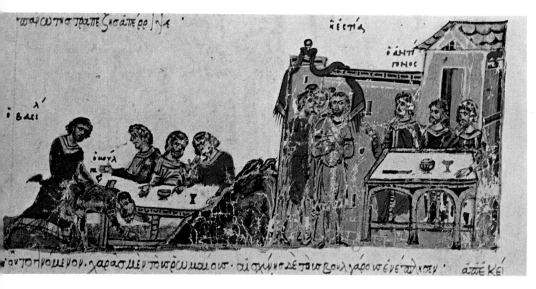

The Emperor himself first heard of the newcomer to Constantinople when, at a banquet, some visiting Bulgarians boasted of the prowess of a wrestler among them. Theophilitzes asked permission to send for his servant, Basil, who easily lifted the Bulgarian and threw him on a table (above, left)—to the delight of all the guests.

While visiting Greece with Theophilitzes, Basil met the rich and lovely widow Danielis, who gave him dinners (left) and presents of slaves and money to buy farms for his Macedonian relatives.

In return she had him take vows of "spiritual brotherhood" (right) with her son, John, for a monk told her Basil would one day be emperor and she hoped he would not forget his friends.

On a hunting trip back in Constantinople, the Emperor's dappled horse ran away and Basil asked Theophilitzes if he might "jump into the imperial saddle and grasp the purple reins." Granted permission, Basil dashed after the runaway (top right), vaulted from one saddle to the other and brought the horse back (bottom). The Emperor appointed him one of his guards.

On another hunting expedition—but now with Basil riding ahead and carrying the imperial mace—the Emperor was attacked by a monstrous wolf that came leaping from the underbrush. With one deadly throw of the mace Basil split the wolf's head in two. As cheers arose for Basil, Caesar Bardas, the Emperor's uncle and his chief advisor, murmured prophetically: "I believe that our family will be exterminated by this man."

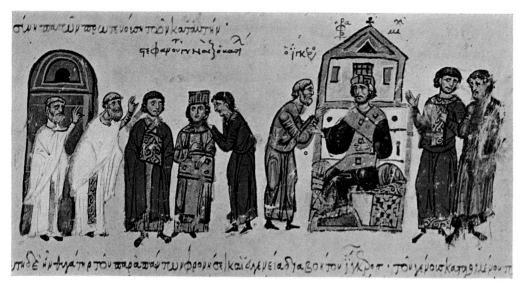

Basking in Michael's favor, Basil was made Grand Chamberlain and was presented with a wife, Eudoxia Ingerina, who also happened to be Michael's mistress. In the picture they are being married (far left), while the Emperor consults Eudoxia's father (center) and Bardas (right) frets with a friend.

Alarmed by Basil's growing power, Michael's mother, the Dowager Empress Theodora, warned her son against him. Here she is being reassured by Michael, who says Basil is loyal to the imperial family. To the left of the Empress, listening with an interested air, is none other than Basil himself.

Seeking to consolidate his position, Basil persuaded Michael to do away with Bardas, Basil's rival, while on a campaign in Asia Minor. After the foul deed was done between battles, Michael led his army home (far left), resumed his throne (center) and had Basil crowned as his co-emperor (right).

The imperial partnership of Michael and Basil ended when Michael found a new favorite, Basiliskianos, a handsome sailor. In drunken folly one night the haloed Emperor dressed this man in royal robes, crowned him and called in priests and officials to bless and pledge loyalty to the new "monarch."

Now Michael also plotted to kill Basil, who had spoken out against the Emperor's drunken excesses. But one of the plotters (far left) spilled the story into Basil's ear and Basil decided to strike first. In the scene at the right, Basil's own assassin bursts into Michael's room and kills him with a sword.

On a litter borne in relay by 300 youths, the widow Danielis comes to see her friend, now sole Emperor of Byzantium. Basil entitled her "Mother of the Emperor," and installed his "spiritual brother" John in high office. Again, she had gifts for Basil: 500 slaves, 100 eunuchs, and silver and rugs.

The campaigns of Basil
were epics of their times,
waged with a refined cruelty
that included tortures
for friend and foe alike

Basil warred against the Arabs almost without interruption through his reign, with the help of able—and cruel—generals. Rarely did he have to chide them for failures such as that shown in the painting at right. In Italy two of his commanders, Leo and Procopius, quarreled and in battle failed to support each other. As a result, Procopius, shown mortally wounded in the center of the picture, was defeated. Knowing Basil would not be pleased, Leo rallied his own and Procopius' forces, and took Tarentum and much booty. Nevertheless he felt the force of Basil's ire (below).

Brought before the Emperor for deserting a fellow commander in battle, Leo is condemned by the pointing finger of Basil (right). In two later scenes (left) Leo suffers his penalty. First he lies on the ground while the official torturer burns out his right eye with a red hot iron. Then, seated, he presents his hand on a piece of wood while the torturer prepares to chop it off at the wrist. Surprisingly, Leo recovered from all of this and lived on to a ripe old age, although in exile and no longer on the imperial payroll.

ὸν τὸν ἀχειματεσσον ·

ὁ πρόκοπος

ἀτερκιοι

ερ γάδαδαι λαμτρὸν · Καὶ τὸ ἐκ τῆς σε ριδος σιοκιάσαι συνιμάνᾶ

πρικιοσ νικηται ταισ ωργας τονγελωντα διαρκνονι · τιμωριαισ διαφοροισ εβαλει

ΙΤ ΛΕΒΙ

ισ μερ. τηνυ τησ σαρκοσ οδραν αφαιρουμενος · Καὶ μαλλουντο σαρνιιαλιενοισ το βατισματουχν · του

One of Basil's favorite officers was Admiral Nicetas Oryphas, who surprised and captured an Arab fleet in the Gulf of Corinth by transporting his ships over the isthmus from the Saronic Gulf. In this painting, Oryphas attempts to dissuade other Arab sailors from further invasions by performing various torments on his prisoners. At his direction, one is being hanged from a forked post; another is being skinned alive; a third is being used for target practice and a fourth is being lowered into boiling tar.

Conspiracies filled Basil's declining years. One plot aroused the emperor against the heir to his throne, but an odd counterplot saved the young man from the ruler's terrible wrath.

Basil distrusted Leo, officially his son but some say the son of Eudoxia and Michael. Hoping to please Basil, a scheming monk (above) decides to trick Leo. He advises him to carry a knife in his boot to protect his father—and then (picture at right) hurries off to tell Basil.

At a banquet, senators friendly to Leo launch an odd but successful appeal to restore him to good grace. They place above Basil a parrot, who pathetically cries, "Ouch! Ouch! Sir Leo," at which the diners fall silent and refuse to eat until Basil relents.

Finally restoring the innocent Leo to freedom and honor, Basil orders him to take off his "vestments of sadness" and have his hair, which had grown long in prison, cut. After this Basil, forgiving all, appointed Leo his heir and successor.

When Basil died—of a wild boar wound suffered on a hunt—the widow Danielis, now very old, made still another trip to pay homage to Leo (right), the son of her spiritual son—and later added her own vast fortune to the new Emperor's inheritance.

The scheming monk informs Basil that Leo is preparing to murder him and therefore he can in good conscience get rid of Leo first. The Emperor can prove Leo's guilt, the monk declares, by having him take off his footwear and seeing whether or not he is armed for the attempt.

On the hunting field Basil announces that he needs a knife, and Leo all innocently whips out the one hidden in his boot and offers it to the Emperor. He is then stripped of the imperial purple and thrown into jail by the angry ruler, who contemplates having Leo's eyes burned out.

4

AN EMPEROR UNDER GOD

Constantine's espousal of Christianity brought with it a change in the status of the emperor who ruled Byzantium. Although the imperial throne retained the magnificence which had surrounded it in the time of Constantine's predecessors—the ceremonial perquisites of emperors like Diocletian who had ruled the Roman Empire as gods—the rulers of the new Christian empire were now regarded not as divine in themselves but only as the chief representatives of Christ and of God Himself.

Yet in another sense the Byzantine emperors were identical with their God: they were His visible manifestation. The invisible activity of God, as everyone knew, consisted in bringing all heavenly principalities into an ordered harmony under His absolute rule. His *visible* activity, carried out by the emperor, was to bring all mankind into an ordered harmony within a universal state under the absolute rule of the monarchy. In this way human society was to imitate divine society. As God was the regulator of the cosmic order, the immovable center around which all revolved, so must the emperor, His human extension, be the regulator of the social order, the immovable center around which all human affairs revolved.

It followed that all the actions of the emperor, as well as his office, had a sacred and symbolic character. His life was surrounded by a ritual that was meant to copy, as nearly as possible, the invisible ritual performed in heaven by God and the divine powers. Thus the emperor's status as an individual was of secondary importance. What was important was that he fulfill the traditional pattern of ceremony that went with his office. Everything was bound up with this: his crown, his throne, his palace, his court, his vestments, his public appearances, his statues, his images, the mystical procession of his days, his imperial service, his pronouncements and his laws.

Although the whole apparatus of elaborate ceremonial, derived in large part from the East, was used to invest the emperor in office, this by no means assured the ruler that his offspring would succeed him—or even that he himself would hold power for long. There was no absolute law binding succession to the throne. Legitimate dynastic descent did give a male candidate strong claims, espe-

GOD'S SPOKESMAN, *the Emperor John Cantacuzene announces religious dogma to bishops and monks at a church council in 1351. The emperors, who usually oversaw church affairs, were often challenged by strong patriarchs.*

UNLUCKY EMPERORS

Violence ended the reigns of 29 Byzantine emperors, including Nicephorus II, whose head was put on public display (above). Other unfortunate rulers are listed below with the dates when disaster struck.

BASILICUS	477	Starved in prison
ZENO	491	Buried alive
MAURICE	602	Decapitated
PHOCAS	610	Dismembered
HERACLEONAS	641	Mutilated
CONSTANTINE III	641	Poisoned
CONSTANS II	668	Bludgeoned in his bath
LEONTIUS	705	Decapitated
TIBERIUS III	705	Decapitated
JUSTINIAN II	711	Decapitated
PHILIPPUCUS	713	Blinded
CONSTANTINE VI	797	Blinded
LEO V	820	Stabbed, decapitated
MICHAEL III	867	Stabbed
CONSTANTINE VII	959	Poisoned
ROMANUS II	963	Poisoned
NICEPHORUS II	969	Stabbed, decapitated
JOHN I	976	Poisoned
ROMANUS III	1034	Poisoned, drowned
MICHAEL V	1042	Blinded
ROMANUS IV	1071	Poisoned, blinded
ALEXIUS II	1183	Strangled, decapitated
ANDRONICUS I	1185	Mutilated and tortured
ISAAC II	1193	Blinded
ALEXIUS IV	1204	Strangled
ALEXIUS V	1204	Blinded, maimed
JOHN IV	1261	Blinded
ANDRONICUS IV	1374	Blinded
JOHN VII	1374	Blinded

cially after the 11th Century, but there was no guarantee of succession. Indeed, the whole idea that an emperor was chosen by divine decree meant that there could be no fixed constitutional rule in this matter. The divine will might express itself in many ways. The only certain method of knowing the divine will was to see who actually occupied the throne. In other words, all means of becoming an emperor were legitimate—so long as they were successful. An unsuccessful attempt to reach the throne, on the other hand, was unforgivable and disastrous for the would-be ruler.

Furthermore, what God had given He could also take away. An emperor's throne might be seized from him in as unpredictable and sudden a manner as it had been given to him in the first place—and the consequences for him were usually as terrible as if he had tried to seize power and failed.

This view of the throne explains the atmosphere of plot and counterplot that shadows the lengthy history of Byzantine royalty. Of the 88 emperors who reigned from 324 to 1453—from Constantine I to Constantine XI—29 died violent deaths, and another 13 took refuge, temporarily or for the rest of their lives, in monasteries.

One emperor who died violently was Nicephorus II Phocas. The ascetic old general was the conqueror of Aleppo, Crete and Antioch, and scourge of the Saracens. He was acclaimed emperor by his troops in 963 after the death of the incumbent, Romanus II, under suspicious circumstances, and soon afterward he married Romanus' young widow, the beautiful Theophano. But Nicephorus was old and unattractive, and before long Theophano had made herself the mistress of one of Nicephorus' former comrades in arms, John Tzimisces, and was busily plotting the death of the Emperor. A party led by Tzimisces was admitted by Theophano's women into the seashore palace where the Emperor was lying asleep. He was stabbed to death and decapitated. His body was pitched out into the snow, and without delay Tzimisces placed himself on the Byzantine throne.

Possibly the most hideous of all imperial deaths was that meted out to Andronicus I Comnenus in 1185. He was chained for days in a pillory and beaten black and blue; his teeth were broken with hammers and one of his hands was cut off. He was then tied to the back of a sick camel and paraded through the streets of Constantinople. Finally, after boiling water had been thrown in his face and an eye had been plucked out, he was strung up for additional torture in the Hippodrome. Over and over he repeated, "Lord have mercy upon me. Why do you strike a broken reed?" He was at last put out of his misery by a sword plunged into his entrails.

Until natural or violent death overtook him, the emperor had to follow the ritual pattern that had developed in Byzantium over the centuries. This ritual is perhaps best described in a vast manual of procedures, *De ceremoniis*, compiled by Constantine VII Porphyrogenitus (913-959). The palace was the stage within which the daily round of solemnities unfolded. Early in the morning the gate leading to the main public square, the Augustaeum, was opened and the captain of the watch would wake the emperor with three knocks on the door of his private apartment.

On official occasions the emperor would wear a long, white, tight-sleeved tunic of silk. Over this he had a purple cape or *chalmys*, opening on the right side and decorated in back and front with embroidered squares of gold cloth, as shown in the portrait of Justinian in the Church of San Vitale at Ravenna. The imperial diadem was a hemispherical, close-fitting cap profusely adorned with pearls and other jewels, some inserted in the crown and some hanging down as far as the nape of the neck. Scarlet shoes embroidered with jewels completed his attire. After dressing, the emperor would emerge,

attended by eunuchs known as *cubicularii*, or officers of the royal wardrobe. He would pray before the icon of Christ and then—presumably after breakfasting—would enter one of the throne rooms.

If an important event was scheduled—the reception of the envoys of a powerful foreign prince, for example—special arrangements would have been made. We have the record of an audience given in the 10th Century to the Arab ambassadors from Tarsus. It was held in the great hall of the Magnaura Palace. The room was lit by great golden candelabra hung from silvered chains of copper. The floors were covered with ivy and laurel, rosemary and roses; as they were trampled underfoot their crushed essence filled the air with sweet perfume. Costly Persian carpets lay at the entrance. On either side of the throne stood the *candidatoi*, imperial guards drawn from noble families, dressed in white and carrying scepters. A choir was stationed above to chant the acclamations. The Arab envoys entered the imperial presence wearing robes specially ordered for them by the emperor.

We also have an account by Liutprand, future Bishop of Cremona, of his reception by Constantine VII Porphyrogenitus in the same hall. Constantine sat in the animated "throne of Solomon." As Liutprand, escorted by two eunuchs, approached the Emperor, the machinery of the throne went into operation: mechanical birds sang and lions roared. Nothing daunted (for he had been forewarned), Liutprand made his prescribed three prostrations before the throne. When he rose to his feet he found that throne and Emperor had disappeared. Glancing upward, he saw both—the Emperor now clad in robes even more magnificent than he had worn when Liutprand entered—hovering near the ceiling. It was with the Emperor in this position that Liutprand had to continue his audience.

Receptions of this kind took place in both morning and afternoon. In the evening there might be a

THEODORA   ZOE   IRENE

THREE FAMOUS EMPRESSES *of Byzantium, portrayed in the mosaics above, led vastly different lives. Theodora, an actress and courtesan before marrying Justinian I, became a trusted adviser to her husband. Zoë, a capricious blonde, inherited the throne, married three times, and spent much of her time beautifying herself. Irene, the daughter of a sainted Hungarian king, devoted herself to charity and herself became a saint.*

banquet. This was sometimes held in a large hall known as the Tribunal of the Nineteen Couches, for it was still the fashion on special occasions for diners to recline on couches in the Roman style. With such a banquet, and the entertainment that went with it—perhaps Greek dancing with one course, readings from St. John Chrysostom with the next, Hindu jugglers to close the show—the emperor's day would end.

The ruler's ceremonial life was as rich and varied as those of rulers in any epoch. He had a whole series of public functions to perform, all similarly cocooned in brilliant pageantry. Perhaps the most spectacular of these were related to the empire's military enterprises. Since the monarch, as Christ's vice-regent on earth, was defender and champion of the faith, every military expedition had something of the character of a sacred war, and ceremonies connected with it were equally solemn.

An occasion for such brilliant display might be provided by a review of the troops before they set out against some invading host, Russian or Bulgar or Persian. The usual parade ground was near the apex of the Golden Horn, at the termination of the great walls enclosing the city to the northwest. All the palaces and towers and churches would be hung with banners, many of them bearing the imperial eagle. The emperor would be rowed up the Golden Horn in his royal galley with its figurehead of an eagle and with gold-emblazoned gonfalons borne aloft. The troops would be drawn up: Dalmatians under their national flags, clothed in their brilliantly embroidered dress, armed with swords and lances; the imperial guards, the *scholarii*, some clothed in rose-colored tunics; another body of royal guards, the great *hetairia*, with swords, silver belts, gilded shields and double-edged axes. Around the emperor himself, as he disembarked, would cluster the famous Varangian Guard—in the earlier years Russians but in later years chiefly Anglo-

Saxons—great flaxen-haired, ax-wielding warriors.

An even more impressive scene would be provided by the triumphant return of the emperor from war. He would ride his white horse through the Golden Gate into the city. Then he would pass with his brilliant escort down the flower-strewn highway, between houses hung with great Babylonian tapestries and Persian embroideries, to the square of the Augustaeum. Here Patriarch and Prefect would welcome him. Later would come the great pageant in the Forum of Constantine or in the Hippodrome. All the captives taken in the war would be paraded before the emperor and the high dignitaries of the court. The imperial chanters would intone paeans of victory. At the climax the emperor would place his scarlet boot on the shaved head of the chief prisoner, perhaps a barbarian king or Persian emir, while all the other prisoners lay prostrate on the ground and the first imperial chanter sang, "Who is great like our God? You are the God who performs miracles."

In palace and public ceremonies the empress too had a part to play. Far from being cloistered in some impenetrable quarter of the palace, she was an adjunct to the emperor on official occasions, and frequently exercised a great deal of authority in her own right.

How the empress was selected is itself of interest. Traditionally, when the time came for the emperor to marry, a group of delegates would be dispatched from the capital to search throughout Byzantine territories for a suitable bride. Candidates had not only to offer a suitable degree of beauty and decorum—wealth and rank were not so important—but they had also to fulfill specific requirements regarding such details as the measurements of the bust, waist and feet. Those who passed this preliminary examination would then be summoned to Constantinople and paraded before the emperor. Like Paris, he would hand an apple to the girl of his choice. (Not all empresses, of course, were cho-

sen in this way. Justinian's wife Theodora was one notable exception.)

The story is told of one girl, supreme in beauty and intelligence, who lost the throne by speaking out of turn. As the emperor was about to hand her the apple, he lamented that it was through women that evil had entered the world. She retorted that it was also through women that what was greater than evil had entered the world—the reference being to the birth of Christ. Such ready wit startled the emperor, who hastily moved farther down the line of aspirants. The young lady, Casia, later became a nun and a poet of high distinction, achieving a reputation for sensitivity and religious fervor.

The empress was virtually mistress of her own court in the women's quarters of the palace, with ladies in waiting and her own host of servitors and dignitaries. Like the emperor, she gave audiences and held banquets, and she conferred gifts on ladies of the court and visiting princesses. She had her own private fortune to administer as she would. In addition to exerting a decisive influence on public affairs, the empress on occasion even served as the sole ruler.

Certain empresses were renowned for their piety —or for their eccentricity. Among these ladies was Zoë (1028-1050), who after 50 years of life in obscurity came to the throne upon the death of her uncle, Constantine VIII. Though rather past the prime of life, this empress was still a striking woman; Psellus, who was never loath to disparage the qualities of Byzantine rulers, wrote that, like a well-baked chicken, "every part of her was firm and in good condition."

Zoë determined not only to make the best possible use of her charms while she still possessed them but also to preserve them by the most advanced scientific means. With typically Byzantine technical ingenuity, she transformed her private apartments into a laboratory full of pipes and braziers and other apparatus for the preparation of unguents. Thus she was able to keep her face free of wrinkles until she was well past her sixtieth summer. Using her beauty to good effect, she found herself three personable husbands who ran the empire (with the assistance of Byzantium's superb corps of civil servants). Only in her late sixties would she admit to herself that age was upon her and begin to spend as much time with her devotions as she had with her chemicals. She died in her 72nd year, serene and still beautiful.

Yet Byzantine empresses as a group seem no more prone to folly or self-indulgence than other ladies; indeed, many of them, like Justinian's Theodora, were strong and effective personages who helped maintain the authority of the throne. Among these one of the most notable was Irene, wife of John II Comnenus (1118-1143), who founded the great monastery of St. Savior Pantocrator, where many Byzantine monarchs were later buried.

For all Byzantines, however, the true ruler of the empire was not an emperor or an empress but Christ Himself. It was His word, as manifested in the Gospels, that provided the ultimate authority; His Cross was carried at the front of military processions; His image, crowned with the imperial diadem, was imprinted on coins; it was in His name, "The Lord Jesus Christ, our Master," that laws were promulgated. The emperor was merely His temporal instrument for guiding the people into the fold of His Kingdom.

That is why everything connected with the imperial office, from the public appearances down to the royal inkpot, was regarded as having a sacred character. Everything was dedicated to the service of God. Not only was the person of the emperor sacred, but so too was all he touched—his garments, his letters, the golden imperial seal. To insult him was to blaspheme. To plot against him was to invite excommunication. Rebellion, if not successful, was apostasy, and deserved the punishment of death. This sanctity also embraced the emperor's ministers: for just as God had to act through the cohorts of angels, the ranks of the superterrestrial powers, so His earthly representative, the emperor, had to act through a corresponding hierarchy of court dignitaries, through the numberless ranks of officials, civil and military, who had to do his bidding on land and sea. Entrance into public office was a kind of ordination; to leave it was to lay down a sacred trust.

It is this hieratic character of the imperial service that accounts both for its centralization and its proficiency, which made it the backbone of the theocratic state. Like much else in Byzantium the imperial bureaucracy was inherited directly from Rome. Down to Heraclius' day (610-641) it used Latin as its official language and preserved Latin titles for its senior officials—*praetorian prefect, magister militum, quaestor sacri palatii,* and so on. But from the Seventh Century onward the service gradually assumed a new form. The Greek language, which had been taking over since the Sixth Century, became official. Greek designations replaced the Latin titles of ministers and high officials—the *spatharioi,* the *protespatharoi,* the *logothetes,* the *strategoi.*

Though careers were always open to all men of talent, generally these functionaries were recruited, after having passed difficult examinations, from distinguished families with a tradition of public service. Officials were nominated, promoted and dismissed by the emperor. They were his representatives, responsible to him for the implementation of his personal wishes, which were the law of the state. The policies they carried out were formulated at the imperial palace, where the emperor met with his council of advisors. High government officials were given honorific court titles so that they would have rank and precedence in the im-

RAISED ON A SHIELD, *a Biblical David is crowned in Byzantine fashion by his army in a scene from a 10th Century manuscript. David, a king chosen by divine decree, became a favorite symbol for Byzantium's theocratic emperors.*

perial household. Since the emperor himself was directly in touch with the heads of government departments, there was no formal provision for an office such as that of prime minister.

For many centuries, however, the chief minister at the court was the *magister officii*, or master of offices. He was head of the entire civil service, the secret police and the state postal system, as well as being responsible for court ceremonies and audiences, including the reception of foreign envoys. The civil service was organized along military lines. Its members wore uniforms, marked with badges indicating their office and rank. A military-style belt was the emblem of the civil service: entering the service was termed "taking the belt," leaving it was to "give up the belt."

After the initiation of the theme system by the Emperor Heraclius early in the Seventh Century, the administration of the empire's provinces became increasingly militaristic. At the head of each theme, or military province, was a general, the *strategos*, who had almost unlimited power in local affairs. He was appointed by the emperor and was responsible to him. As a check against any abuse of power on the part of the military governor, a civilian was named to serve alongside him, though in a subordinate position; he too was in direct communication with the emperor.

The Byzantines were not by nature militaristic. It was the need to defend the empire against the many enemies who coveted its wealth that prompted Byzantium to mold itself along military lines. Its army was not very large—at its peak it probably numbered only some 120,000 men—but it was expensive to maintain. Much attention was therefore paid to the development of military strategy in order to avoid a waste of lives and equipment. In Constantine's time, the Roman army was already moving away from the legionary system, which was proving increasingly dangerous and ineffective: dangerous because the legionaries would depose an emperor; ineffective because these infantrymen were no match for barbarian cavalry. A new form of organization emerged, consisting of a frontier force of settled soldier-farmers who gave part-time military service, plus a mobile central force which could be deployed wherever needed. Foot soldiers were normally equipped with spears, swords and shields. The more important heavy cavalry wore steel caps, shirts of mail reaching to the thighs, gauntlets and steel shoes, and were armed with long lances, spears and broadswords, bows and arrows. The other component of the armed forces, the fleet, was held in lower esteem than the army, though it was vital in the defense of Constantinople against Arab attacks.

Since diplomacy was cheaper than war as a means of self-protection, it was zealously pursued. There was no formal provision for a diplomatic service within the imperial government's structure. But it was well understood by those who served along the borders or who otherwise came into contact with foreigners that Byzantium's international position was to be actively safeguarded by all peaceful means. Byzantine diplomacy, as it developed from this assumption, was, on the one hand, marvelously formal, involving the most sumptuous of gifts and the most lavish of ceremonial receptions; it was on the other hand, perceptive, realistic, and full of underhanded skulduggery. A fairly standard Byzantine maneuver in this kind of subtle warfare was to honor treaty obligations to a neighboring state as a good Christian monarch should, but to undermine that state by subsidizing and equipping its enemies and inciting them to attack.

Marriage was yet another Byzantine diplomatic weapon: noble ladies were sent to foreign courts to marry and civilize distant monarchs, and alien brides were often brought to the imperial throne. Other elements in the life of the court that be-

spoke the empire's strenuous diplomatic activity were kings and queens in exile, biding their time until a cleverly arranged coup might put them back on their thrones (supported by regular emoluments from Constantinople, of course), and wide-eyed ambassadors from the ends of the known world who were being led from office to office through the maze of imperial intrigue.

Many of the highest offices in Byzantium were held by eunuchs. Since a eunuch could not be emperor—and could not, of course, pass on hereditary rights—this often made advancement easier for such men. As a consequence, the Byzantines attached no disgrace to castration; noblemen would often castrate their sons in order to further their chances of advancement and success. At least one emperor, Romanus I, castrated both his legitimate and his illegitimate sons in order to fit them better for the high offices he wished them to occupy. Patriarchs of Constantinople were frequently eunuchs, and so also were commanders in the army or the navy. Narses, Justinian's famous general, was a eunuch, and so was Eustathius Cymineanus, the admiral appointed by Alexius I. If one wanted to become a fashionable doctor it was an advantage, for only eunuchs or women doctors could treat women.

It was in the civil service that eunuchs were particularly favored; here they took precedence, and many senior posts were reserved exclusively for them. The presence of eunuchs in the high ranks of the imperial service, operating as a check on any tendency for power to fall into the hands of a hereditary nobility, may have been one cause of the stability and reliability of the Byzantine administrative system.

As an autocratic establishment, this system was expensive, cumbersome and liable to corruption. But for more than 11 centuries it served the emperors well as they sought to hold together the many contradictory realities of the empire.

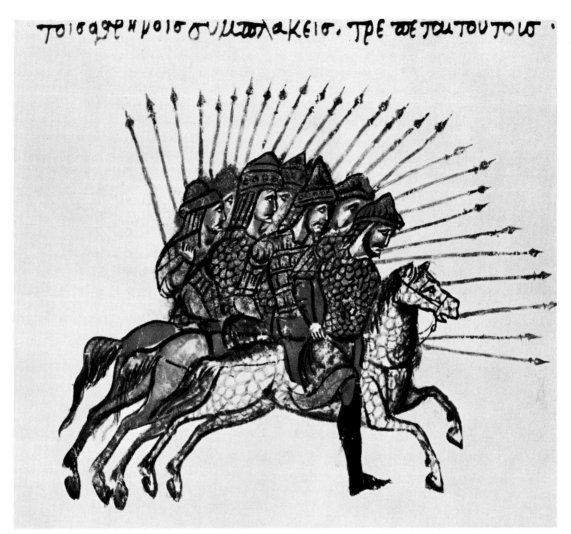

CHARGING CAVALRYMEN, *their mounts wheeling in a tightly disciplined maneuver, bring a fan of spears to bear on the enemy.*

TECHNIQUES OF WAR

Although the Byzantines usually preferred diplomacy to bloodshed, they could wage highly scientific warfare when they had to. As the heirs of the invincible Roman legions and the defenders of Christendom, the army regarded itself, and rightly so, as the best fighting force in the world. Its officers were schooled in geography and strategy, and even emperors wrote manuals on tactics. While their enemies often blundered onto the field, the Byzantines moved their infantry and cavalry—the fighting edge of the land forces—through complex and orderly maneuvers *(above)*. The men in the front lines were backed by a host of auxiliaries: servants, scouts, guards for the supply train and an ambulance corps which rescued the wounded and gathered up the spoils. There was even an intelligence service, the "Office of Barbarians," that collected information about the Saracens, Turks and Bulgars who ringed the empire, and advised generals on strategy.

ARCHERS ON HORSEBACK

A HORSE-ARCHER *turns in his saddle to take aim.*

In the Byzantine army, the cavalry was supreme. During the empire's height, from the Seventh to the 12th Centuries, cavalrymen, like other Byzantine soldiers, were career professionals. They were also the best trained and most highly paid fighters in the world. In battle, the first assault wave was almost always a detachment of archers mounted on horses; it was their task to harry and break the enemy's ranks. Behind them came a second line of armored lancers who rode in for closer combat. Shooting accurately with a bow while on horseback required long training, and most of the mounted bowmen were recruited from among the tribes of Asia Minor, who were renowned for their horsemanship and fighting skill.

SPEAR IN HAND, *an infantryman starts on a march.*

INFIGHTERS ON FOOT

Foot soldiers, who had been the mainstay of the Roman land forces, played a secondary but vital role in the Byzantine army. Ordinarily, the infantry did not serve in the front lines because Byzantium's chief enemies, the Turks and Saracens, were entirely mounted. However, when the Byzantines fought armies of foot soldiers, such as the Slavs and the Franks, the infantry came into its own. It also took precedence in battles fought in hilly country or in narrow passes where horses did not have enough space to maneuver. Foot soldiers also handled the less glamorous tasks: fortifying the camp every night by digging a deep ditch around it, guarding the wagon train carrying supplies, and holding mountain passes and river fords to block an enemy retreating before the hard-riding Byzantine cavalry.

A CAVALRYMAN'S UNIFORM *(left) consisted of scale armor, under which he wore a linen tunic in summer and a woolen tunic in winter. Over his shoulders he draped a felt cloak that served as a raincoat and a blanket, and as camouflage to cover his gleaming armor during night attacks. His weapons included a bow and arrows, a small round shield, a broadsword, a battle-ax and a lance almost 12 feet long. His saddle was equipped with stirrups—a revolutionary device the Byzantines started employing in the Sixth Century. Stirrups gave the rider a firm seat and allowed him to slash with his sword, or thrust with his lance, without falling off his mount.*

AN INFANTRYMAN'S WEAPONS *(right) included a larger bow than the cavalryman's and a shorter broadsword for hand-to-hand fighting, as well as a sling, a mace, a short javelin and a long pike. The mace's edges were honed sharp enough to cut through a metal helmet when brought down in an overhead swing. The front line of the infantry was usually armored like the cavalry, but since armor was extremely expensive, the men sometimes wore only a helmet. An infantryman ordinarily carried a round or oval shield larger than that of the cavalryman. As in the cavalry, each regiment could be identified by the distinctive colors painted on its shields.*

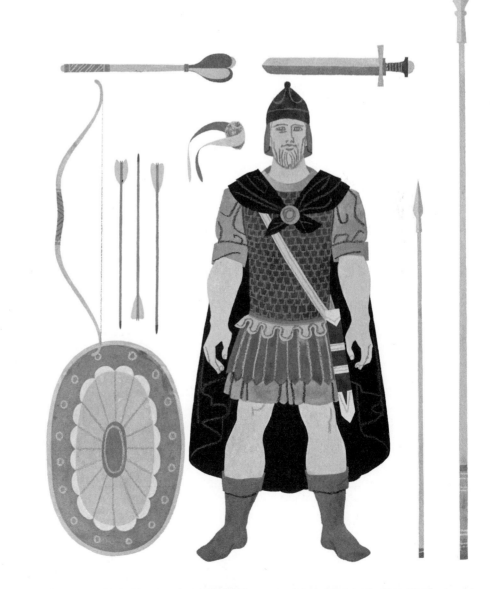

ENGINEERING A SIEGE

Byzantium was seldom secure enough militarily that it could afford to stage an all-out offensive war, but its armies sometimes laid siege to individual enemy strongholds. First the artillery set up a line of mangons *(below)*, medium-sized catapults that hurled heavy stones (and sometimes, to entertain the bored besiegers, live mules or dead enemy soldiers) over the fortress walls. When the missiles had driven enough of the defenders from their posts along the ramparts, the Byzantine troops moved in to hammer the gates with battering rams or bore holes through the walls with huge, metal-tipped drills. A less obvious, but often more effective, siege technique was mining. Soldiers would dig a tunnel under the city walls, shoring up the burrow with timbers as they went. When they had finished digging, they would soak the timbers in oil, set them on fire, and scramble back through the tunnel. Unless the enemy could put the fire out in time, the shoring would burn away, the wall above it would collapse into the tunnel, and the Byzantine forces would stream in through the breach.

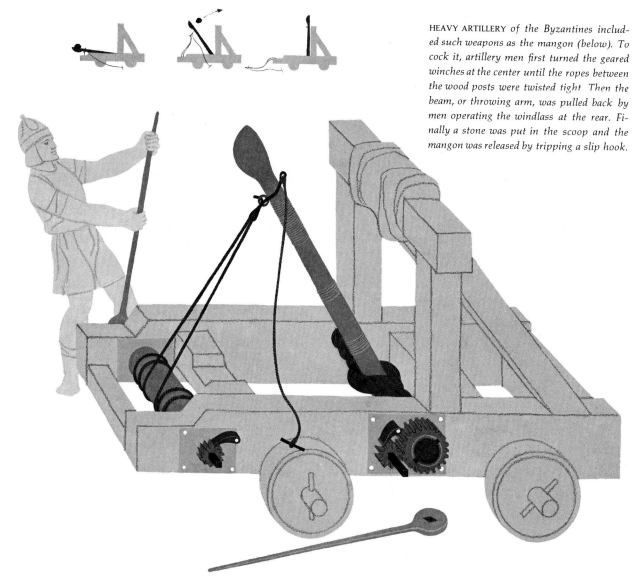

HEAVY ARTILLERY *of the Byzantines included such weapons as the mangon (below). To cock it, artillery men first turned the geared winches at the center until the ropes between the wood posts were twisted tight. Then the beam, or throwing arm, was pulled back by men operating the windlass at the rear. Finally a stone was put in the scoop and the mangon was released by tripping a slip hook.*

TWO TYPES OF DRILL, *apparently designed for boring straight through fortress walls, are shown in a miniature from an 11th Century Byzantine treatise on siegecraft. Two soldiers rotate the upper drill, which is held steady in a socket, by turning long handles attached to it. The drill below, probably the artist's own inventive design, was operated by men sawing a huge bow back and forth.*

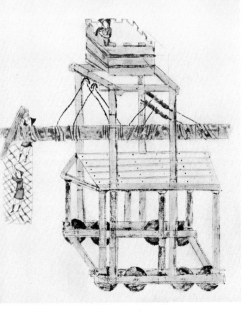

SCALING THE WALLS, *the soldier at far left mounts a ladder to a net held by grappling hooks thrown over the battlements. In the picture at right two besiegers climb a similar net hung from a battering ram. The ram, a large tree trunk tipped with metal, is swung on ropes from a movable tower, which has a heavy lower roof to shield the soldiers pushing it and a small fort to protect archers on top.*

SHIPBORNE BRIDGES *are maneuvered up to the walls of a fortress. The one at right is a battering ram, fitted with railings so that soldiers can cross it. Both bridges have been hoisted to the height of the ramparts and are being shoved forward so that they can lie on top of the walls. The heads on the platforms may be symbolic decorations, or weights to keep the top-heavy structures steady.*

MANNING A FLAME-GUN, *a soldier stands on a scaling ladder and releases a stream of Greek fire on an enemy fortress. The gun, which was essentially a piston in a cylinder, worked like a small hand pump or syringe. The Byzantines also used such flame-throwing weapons for defense; the Emperor Constantine VII ordered them used "against any tower that may be advanced against the wall of a besieged town."*

FIERY GUNS AND SHIPS

The most terrifying single weapon the Byzantines had was a mysterious liquid called "Greek fire." When squirted from tubes or thrown in clay pots, Greek fire would ignite spontaneously and burn even on water. Its main ingredients are thought to have been naphtha, sulphur and saltpeter, mixed in proportions that were a state secret; the exact formula was never written down.

The Byzantines learned how to make Greek fire in the Seventh Century and at first used it both on land and at sea. The slightest shock in conveying Greek fire overland, however, caused it to explode, and it was eventually reserved almost exclusively for naval battles. Equipped with the deadly weapon the fleet controlled the Mediterranean, and time and again the fiery liquid averted impending defeats. Russia's Prince Igor might have captured Constantinople in 941 if Greek fire had not been turned against his 10,000 ships—all of which reportedly burst into flames and sank.

A SHIP OF THE LINE *called a dromon, or "runner,"
had mounted in its bow a high wooden turret from
which projected three tubes for spraying Greek
fire. Just aft were catapults for hurling fiery missiles made of wadded cloth soaked in oil. Each ship
was manned by some 230 oarsmen and 70 marines.*

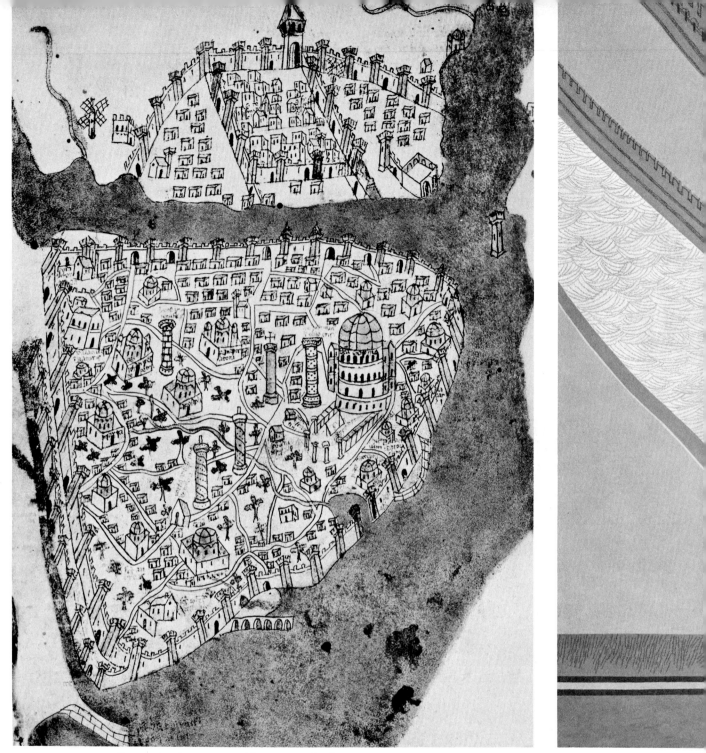

A FORTIFIED PENINSULA, *Constantinople was protected from invasion by the sea, a moat on one side and 13 miles of walls.*

THE CITY WALLS *on the landwar*

THE FORMIDABLE WALLS OF CONSTANTINOPLE

The elaborate defense works that surrounded Constantinople made it in its day the best-fortified city in the world. The walls were erected in the Fifth Century to protect the city against the Goths and Huns, who had captured Rome. They served their purpose well, holding off invaders for nearly a thousand years. As shown in the 15th Century map above, a single wall bounded the city's seaward sides, which were defended by the Byzantine fleet. On the land side, the Byzan-

de rose in levels behind the moat. The towers of the middle and inner walls—192 in all—were staggered in alignment to bring maximum fire against invaders.

tines constructed a moat and three walls that were up to 25 feet thick. As indicated in the sketch *(above right)*, invaders were faced first with a moat some 60 feet wide and 22 feet deep that was normally dry but that could be flooded by pipes. Behind the moat was a low wall to shield a line of archers. Even if the attackers could overcome this first defense, they were confronted by a second wall, 27 feet high, which sheltered more troops. Beyond the second wall lay the third and strongest bulwark. Its towers, some 70 feet high, housed more archers and missile throwers. Only the force of gunpowder finally demolished the protecting walls, bringing Constantinople down. The Turkish Sultan Mehmet II pounded the city for a month and a half with cannon balls weighing as much as 1,200 pounds. Gradually sections of the huge ramparts crumbled, and on May 29, 1453, the capital—and its empire—fell at last before the onrushing Turkish hordes.

5
THE HOLY ESTABLISHMENT

As Constantine approached Rome in 312 A.D. to fight his decisive battle at the Milvian Bridge with Maxentius, the rival Emperor in the West, he is said to have had a revelation. It was a revelation crucial for subsequent European history. Some accounts say Constantine saw a luminous cross in the sky, others say only that he had a dream, as a result of which he was led to inscribe a new sign on his banner. Later this was elaborated into the declaration that he had a vision of the Christian Cross inscribed with the words: "In this sign conquer."

In any case, what Constantine dreamed or saw was a Christian sign, and it was under the protection of this sign that he won his decisive victory. After this battle Constantine counted himself a Christian, and in this spirit he began the process of transforming the pagan empire into a Christian empire, even though he did not himself receive Christian baptism until he was on his deathbed 25 years later. Imperial favor was granted the Christian Church, properties confiscated from it during the time of persecutions were restored, and Christianity's right to legal status was affirmed.

In the very nature of Constantine's conversion lay the seeds of later conflict in the religious structure of Byzantium. For Constantine had not come to Christianity in a normal way. He had come to it—so he believed—through the direct revelation and intervention of God Himself. As the liturgical text from the hymn sung on the day of Constantine's Feast puts it, "Like Paul he received a call not from man." His conversion, moreover, was not like that of a private citizen: it was the conversion of an emperor. This meant that in Constantine's view —and in the view of others who came to believe like him—both the emperor and the imperial structure of which he was the head had been directly chosen and consecrated by God. The emperor and the empire had received a divine blessing and from then on were under the direct protection of the Cross. It soon became clear, however, that if the well-being of the state depended on its submission to its protector, the Cross, then its officials and citizens could not very well hold beliefs that were radically opposed to Christianity. In fact, the persecution of pagans began during Constantine's reign and con-

SAINTS, ANGELS AND EMPERORS *were often depicted together in the art of Byzantium, where Christianity was the state religion. In the 11th Century illumination at left, the Emperor Nicephorus III (center) receives a book of sermons from St. John Chrysostom (left) while the Archangel Michael looks on.*

tinued in the reign of his sons. In 341 pagan sacrifices were forbidden; in 353 the cults of idols were declared illegal and temples were closed; and in the reign of Theodosius the Great (379-395) Christianity was declared the official religion of the state and the faith required of Byzantine citizens.

This adoption of a compulsory state religion was in part the result of a growing need for a strong unifying force in an empire that embraced a diversity of peoples and that was besieged by dissension from within and by barbarian invasions from without. In pagan Rome such a unifying force had been to some extent provided by the practice of emperor worship. Prostration in the presence of an emperor and the burning of incense before his statue were acts of political allegiance to the divine head of state. Could not Christianity now be used to foster unity in somewhat the same way? The Church readily agreed, rejoicing in its new status and tempted by the vision of a Christian society in which men were brought to salvation by law as well as by grace.

In submitting to this temptation, the ministers of the Church were of course forgetting that such a close identification of Church and state was a reversion to pre-Christian practice. The boundaries of the Church's domain had been clearly circumscribed by Christ Himself. Had He not explicitly stated, "My kingdom is not of this world," and had not His life and actions rejected all worldly status and authority? Christianity, therefore, if it were to remain true to its doctrine, could not fully merge itself with the state. Separation of religion from political control was demanded by the very nature of the faith. In Byzantium, the alliance entered into by Church and state was to result in a very complex relationship.

The conflict was not immediately apparent. What was clear was that Christianity, for so long an oppressed religion, had now emerged triumphant. Indeed, it had captured its most bitter persecutor, the Roman state. This could hardly seem anything less than miraculous and providential, a direct manifestation of the Divine Will in the affairs of mankind. But if the Roman Empire was now to be Christian, then a new philosophical framework had to be created to define the nature of its ruler and the source of his power.

The theory put forward by Eusebius, Bishop of Caesarea and one of Constantine's closest ecclesiastical advisors, was so suited to the needs of state and society that it was to endure for more than a millennium, with only minor changes, as the political philosophy of the Byzantine state.

With astute respect for prevailing traditions, Eusebius wove strands taken from Hellenism and Roman practice into a Christian framework. From Hellenism came the concept of the emperor as father, benefactor and savior of his people. From late pagan Rome, where the emperors had ruled as gods, came the exalted status of the ruler, who buttressed his power by adopting a favorite pagan divinity. Now the Christian emperor could claim the Christian God as his source of strength. Such a bond had been forged in Constantine's submission to the Cross on the eve of his victory at the Milvian Bridge, a triumph that made manifest— so the theory went—the designation of Constantine (and his successors on the throne) as the elect of God. Eusebius wrote: "Thus the God of all . . . appointed Constantine . . . to be prince and sovereign, so that while others have been raised to this distinction by the election of their fellow men, he is the only one to whose elevation no mortal man may boast of having contributed." As God's chosen instrument, the emperor was to rule on earth as God's vice-regent and representative. And, since earth was a counterpart of Heaven, the emperor was to play on earth a role analogous to that of God in Heaven. Just as there was one all-powerful ruler in Heaven, so on earth there would be but one absolute monarch—the ruler of the Roman Empire.

This exalted status, however, brought with it responsibilities. It was the emperor's duty to prepare his people for the Kingdom of God and to lead them to it. He was to be answerable to God for the spiritual and temporal welfare of his subjects. He was to rule through the guidance and inspiration of God. So it was that Constantine had himself portrayed on coins: a profile image with eyes directed upward awaiting guidance from Heaven.

Since the emperor's responsibility in religious affairs was thus magnified, it was inevitable that a certain tension would arise between emperor and Church. In cases where the interests and jurisdiction of the two overlapped, which authority should prevail? This vital question remained unresolved through the centuries of Byzantium's existence. On occasion the emperor would assert his claim to supreme authority in religious affairs; at other times the Church would try to establish an ascendancy over the emperor and state.

As far as the Church was concerned, these developments had several consequences. First and foremost, the Christian Church emerged from the catacombs into which it had been driven by the pagan emperors of Rome. Furthermore, if Roman—or Byzantine—society was to evolve into a Christian society, the Church had to have an active social role and be the chief instrument through which this evolution was carried out. To play its new role most effectively, the Church hastened to adapt its organization to that of the empire.

When, under Diocletian, the old Roman provinces had been reorganized into dioceses, the early Christians had adopted the same plan. Bishops were appointed to administer the churches in each diocese, and they were responsible to higher bishops, called metropolitans, who exercised authority in an area larger than the diocese. By Constantine's

THE PARALLEL PATHS OF TWO RELIGIONS

Between the Third and Sixth Centuries, while Christianity was spreading through the Roman and Byzantine Empires, Buddhism moved out from its native India to Central Asia, China and Korea. Although it is doubtful that the two religions influenced each other, their rapid growth followed similar lines. Both gained strong footholds in a time when the existing governments were in sharp decline: Christianity began to flourish as the Roman Empire decayed; Buddhism became strongly rooted in China during the four centuries of confusion following the disintegration of the Han Dynasty in the Third Century—a period during which the gilt bronze Buddha shown above was cast.

The early rise of Buddhism and Christianity had something else in common: both were widely accepted for the spiritual strength they offered people in a time of chaos. The aftermath of this parallel religious expansion was, however, quite different. When the Roman Empire stabilized around Byzantium, Christianity became the official state religion. Buddhism, on the other hand, eventually merged with Taoism and Confucianism into the complex amalgam of Chinese religious thought.

time, the most important metropolitans in the eastern part of the empire were those who presided over the key areas of Alexandria, Antioch, Ephesus, Heraclea and Caesarea. A special place of honor in the Church was held by the bishop of Rome, the successor to Saint Peter, the Prince of the Apostles.

The town of Byzantium, when it was chosen by Constantine as his new capital, was no more than a minor bishopric under the jurisdiction of the metropolitan of Heraclea. So humble a status was clearly unsuitable for the bishops of the administrative center of the Roman Empire, the city of the emperor, Christ's vice-regent on earth. Inevitably, Constantinople assumed a dominant religious position; by 381, scarcely 50 years after the city's dedication in 330, the fathers of the second great Church council declared that the bishop of Constantinople should be accorded primacy of honor among the bishops, second only to the bishop of Rome, because Constantinople was the "New Rome, the city of the emperor and the Senate." A later council, held at Chalcedon in 451, confirmed this hierarchy and in addition allotted to the see of Constantinople the dioceses of Pontus, Asia and Thrace, giving it a status equal to other great religious centers like Antioch and Alexandria.

The religious elevation of the capital reached its peak in the Sixth Century, when Justinian I called the Church at Constantinople "the head of all other churches." Apparently he was also the first to call its bishop—or patriarch, as the heads of the great religious sees came to be called—"ecumenical"—a title against which the Pope of Rome, Gregory, later protested, but which nonetheless became the title by which the patriarch of Constantinople is known to the present day. The explanation is simple: the Byzantine empire was called the *oekumene* (the universe), so it was natural that its senior patriarch should be "ecumenical." The administrative structure of the Church gradually became more centralized, with the bishop of Constantinople at the center, and his representatives—the other bishops —in charge of the administrative subdivisions. In order to make this centralized government of the Church workable, a permanent episcopal synod, or council, was established at Constantinople, presided over by the patriarch. This completed the modeling of the structure of the Byzantine Church on that of the state. As there was an emperor, so there was a patriarch; and as the emperor ruled— at least theoretically—through a senate, so the patriarch ruled through a synod.

Hand in hand with Constantinople's transformation into the religious center of the empire went the attempt to transform the city itself into a "New Jerusalem," an image of Heaven. Constantine the Great had already started this process, not only by setting up Christian symbols in prominent places in the city, but more concretely by building the Church of the Holy Apostles and laying the foundations for the great Church of Hagia Sophia. There seems little doubt that Constantine had a sense of the sacred mission of his city; and this mystical vision of Constantinople as a holy city was to deepen and become more compelling through subsequent centuries.

The most tangible expression of this vision was the multiplying throughout the city of monuments, memorials and various objects connected with the Christian faith. In countless churches, sanctuaries and shrines, all magnificently decorated, lay relics of the new faith, brought in piety, love and devotion from all the provinces of the empire. Through the possession of these relics—the earthly testimonials of the saints now inhabiting Heaven—it was felt that something of Heaven's influence and radiance might be conferred on Constantinople.

The fact that Christianity became the required faith of the empire also meant that the state had a vital concern in defining and preserving Church dogma. Before the time of its alliance with the state, Church regulations had been formulated by local councils that met to deal with general questions of Church organization and dogma as the need arose. These rules were adequate as long as Christianity itself remained a matter of individual belief and worship. But when it became the faith of the emperor—and later the official religion—answers had to be found for a whole host of new questions, varying from the most subtle points of doctrine down to the most ordinary practical details.

This pressure for greater elaboration in matters of Church dogma and discipline resulted in a series of gatherings—known as ecumenical councils—at which emperor and bishops met to debate the points at issue and make the necessary decisions. Generally these councils were summoned by the emperor when doctrinal disputes among his subjects threatened to lead to serious disturbances of the peace and unity of the state. Thus, the First Ecumenical Council met at Nicaea in the spring of 325 in order to pronounce judgment on what was known as Arianism, a set of teachings initiated in Alexandria by the learned presbyter Arius on the nature of the relationship of the Son of God to God the Father. Subsequent ecumenical councils—such as the second held at Constantinople in 381, the third at Ephesus in 431, the great fourth council at Chalcedon in 451, or the seventh one held at Nicaea in 787 —were similarly summoned to deal first of all with theological principles of great complexity concerned with such matters as the Holy Trinity, the meaning of the two natures in Christ, or the place and function of the icon in Christian worship.

The icon was the focus of a particularly long dispute which nearly tore the empire apart. The early Christians, inheriting from Judaism a repugnance toward idolatry, had looked askance at any veneration of pictures of holy persons. But from the Fifth Century on, icons or images—of Christ, the Virgin Mary and the saints—became increasingly prevalent in public and private worship. So fervent, in fact, did the veneration of icons become that it often did border on idolatry. The peoples of the eastern provinces, influenced by their close contact with Moslems and Jews, whose faiths flatly prohibited religious imagery, became alarmed.

A full-scale attack against the religious use of images was launched in 726 when Emperor Leo III, himself of eastern birth, ordered all icons removed from churches and destroyed. He had strong support for this destruction, or iconoclasm, from the army, largely recruited in the eastern provinces, and from the governmental bureaucracy, which was as anxious as the Emperor to curb the growing power of the Church. Ranged in defense of the icon were the peoples of the western provinces and most of the clergy, who regarded iconoclasm as sacrilege and heresy.

The attack upon icons raged for more than half a century. Riots erupted as the factions took their quarrel into the streets; systematic persecutions were visited on the monks, the most vigorous defenders of the icon. In 780 the Empress Irene, a native of the western provinces and an ardent believer in icons, became regent, and in 787 she summoned the Seventh Ecumenical Council. This meeting condemned iconoclasm and drew a distinction between true worship, reserved for God alone, and veneration, or honor given to an icon but in reality transmitted to its holy subject. As a result, icons were once more permitted in churches and public buildings.

These events were followed by a quarter of a century of uneasy peace. Opposition to the restoration of icons was deep-rooted, and in 813, when another eastern Emperor, Leo V, came to the throne, the icons were again removed and a new wave of persecution broke out. This time, however, support for iconoclasm was less enthusiastic and the icon defenders were better organized. When the Empress Theodora became regent she managed to have the monk Methodius, a victim of iconoclast persecution, elected to the patriarchal throne. From the great Church of Hagia Sophia, in the year 843, Methodius proclaimed the final restoration of icons, and iconoclasm, which the Eastern Church regarded as the last of the great heresies, had finally been overcome.

To understand how religious disputes could become so important that they could seriously endanger the security of the empire, one must remember that religion has rarely played as central a role in daily life as it did in Byzantium. Theology was not simply a matter for the experts; it was literally a question of life or death. The prospect of salvation or damnation in the hereafter hinged upon correctness of belief and mode of worship. Nor was dogma the preserve of the clergy, to be propounded to a submissive laity.

Both theology and dogma were the expression of popular consciousness, for which all, from the emperor downward, felt responsible. A revolution, the overthrow of a dynasty, might be incited by the incorrect definition of Christ's nature or interpretation of a ritual gesture. Gaunt, saintly hermits, summoned from their retreats by an indignant populace, might enter Constantinople and actually bring to heel an erring emperor. At the end of the Byzantine period what was perhaps the great majority of the empire's clergy and laity preferred facing conquest by the Turks to accepting help from the Roman West, since they feared that such aid would be dependent on the surrender of certain of their fundamental religious beliefs.

Although the state had a vital interest in religious matters, and although the Church itself was willing to cooperate in the building of the sacred empire, it must not be thought that the Church was simply a subservient tool in the emperor's hands. There were, to be sure, frequent examples of servility among the leaders of the Church, and on many occasions secular interests triumphed temporarily over Christian principles. But in the final analysis the consciousness of these principles was never lost by the Church; though the councils may have been summoned by the emperor, what emerged from them was in fact a crystallization of the inner truth of the Church's faith and experience. Ultimately, the emperor's absolutism was limited by this truth to which both he and his empire were committed, and whose formulation lay ultimately with Christ's apostolic ministers and not with the emperor. Even if the clash between the principles of the Church and those of the state was muted in Byzantium by the Church's acceptance of the notion of a Christian society formed by the state, there were still times when the Church boldly held firm, refusing to betray or compromise the truth for which it stood or the vision of human life and destiny that went with it.

It is difficult in a few words to give an idea of the vision which lay behind all Byzantine religious belief. It would be wrong, however, to overstress its otherworldly or purely transcendental aspects. On the contrary, man himself—the human person—was felt to be very much at the center of things. The individual, Byzantines believed, held the keys to his or her own fate, either to become God-like through the development of innate spiritual potentialities, or to be swept away into outer darkness. Yet however God-like man might become, his destiny was to remain human.

It was not only the human mind that could aspire to a union with God. The human body was also said to have a capacity for experiencing spiritual realities. In fact, everything that existed could participate, simply by reason of its existence, in the highest life of all. The divine energies, as they were

called, were said to be present in everything; to put it another way—everything had its point of contact with the spiritual world. Man himself was felt to be the microcosm of all existing things, of the whole creation; and so his own destiny was very much bound up with that of the rest of creation and with its struggles and suffering. "What is a compassionate heart?" asked one of the spiritual masters of the Byzantine world, Isaac of Nineveh. "It is a heart which burns with compassion for the whole of creation—for men, for birds, for beasts, for demons, for all creatures. He who has this heart cannot call to mind or see one creature without his eyes filling with tears because of the immense compassion which seizes his heart. . . ."

The Byzantine vision of life was also mirrored in its elaborate and intricate church service, the Divine Liturgy. And it was in the liturgy that the corporate life of the Byzantine people found its most complete religious expression. All echelons of society participated in this great sacred drama, which was not simply a ritual spectacle or a representation of past historical events, but a reliving, through the powerful imagery of language, gesture, chant, hymn and invocation, of the central mysteries of the Christian faith. In the course of this drama, emperor, clergy and common folk alike were re-minded that their titles, honors and even citizenship depended not merely on membership in a terrestrial empire but on their commitment to God.

In the endless re-enacting of the Christian mysteries in the liturgy, the empire found its justification and savored its fulfillment. Church and state, clergy and people here made manifest their existence as a single social and political body, a holy nation, chosen under God and dedicated to His service. The celebration of this belief could be awesome indeed. After they had attended services in the Great Church of Hagia Sophia at Constantinople, the envoys sent by Vladimir, Prince of Kiev, told their master: "We know not whether we were in Heaven or on earth, for surely there is no such splendor or beauty anywhere upon earth. We cannot describe it to you; only we know that God dwells there among men, and that their service surpasses the worship of all other places. For we cannot forget that beauty."

In the Byzantine world, however, those who were most concerned with the spiritual life were not the official clergy but the monks and nuns, whose importance cannot be overestimated. The monasteries were not simply refuges for those seeking escape from the hardships of life; they were the forging houses of what the Byzantines regarded as the highest types of humanity. The emperor might be God's elect, but the saint or holy man—especially if he came from some rocky fastness or desert cave—was something more. He was a person who had broken through the barrier between man and God and had restored, or remade, the full integrity of human nature.

This is not to say that all monks and nuns fulfilled the Christian ideal. The cloister held an attraction for all ranks of society. Many entered it devoutly, in search of a life of humility and penitence. Others saw in it a refuge from disgrace, grinding poverty, or the overwhelming burdens of public office. Still others viewed it as a means of attaining high ecclesiastical advancement; in Byzantium, most of the bishops were recruited from the monasteries. Monastic life offered other advantages: monks were exempt from military service, and the monasteries had at their disposal vast tracts of land, which formed the core of their great wealth. Over the centuries, the power of the monasteries grew to such heights that even so pious an emperor as Nicephorus Phocas could not help but be forthright in his description of monastic practices in the 10th Century: "The monks possess none of the evangelical virtues; they think of nothing save the acquisition of land, the erecting of huge buildings and the purchase of vast numbers of horses, cattle, camels and every kind of livestock. All their energies are devoted to their own enrichment, so that their life in no way differs from that of the people living in the world." "What a contrast . . . between this frivolous existence and the lives of the holy [men] who in past centuries dwelt in Egypt, Palestine, and Alexandria, those whose almost immaterialized existence was more that of angels than of men."

But despite its excesses, monasticism lost none of the esteem it held in the eyes of the common people. For them, the monk was a present source of mercy, miracle and guidance, the father of the people among whom he dwelt and the mediator for them between earth and Heaven. Mortal life was a constant war between myriad unseen forces, divine and demoniac. Hemmed in by the demons, tempted and overcome, dragged into misfortune or sickness, where else could a man turn but to those who through divine power could subject even the demons to their bidding? If disease came, the holy man cured the sick with his healing grace. If taxgatherers or landowners attempted to extort or oppress the poor —or even if the emperor himself tried to abuse his office—the ascetic saint was there to defend against the greed and injustice of the powerful. For what had the ascetic to fear at the hands of the mightiest of earthly beings? He had already renounced the world and all its ways. All that could be taken from him now was his mortal life, and if he were to lose that through violence laid upon him, it might well be but to gain a martyr's crown and so to become an even stronger focus of popular worship.

In addition to their spiritual gifts, the monasteries provided most of the fine scribes and artists who created Byzantium's magnificent illuminated manuscripts; who wrote the hymns and composed the liturgical music, so lyrical even in their somber profundity; who made some of the finest mosaics and frescoes. It was through such people as these that the springs of inspiration flowed and to them Byzantium was indebted for much that was most vital in its achievement. Most of the great monastic centers of the Byzantine world, at Constantinople or elsewhere, have now disappeared. But perhaps the greatest of them all, that on Mount Athos, whose earliest existing monastery was founded in 963 by St. Athanasius the Athonite, survives to this present day. It is a living monument to the Byzantine spirit, and a treasure house of countless works of art that testify to the creative fertility of the Byzantine monastic tradition.

THE HERMIT LUKE, *his arms raised in a blessing, looks down on his church. Above him is Saint James.*

A PICTURE-BOOK CHURCH

Everywhere in the empire, Byzantines worshiped in churches that glowed with the subdued and golden light of mosaics. Often every wall, every niche and curving surface was covered with pictures of Biblical events and personalities, pieced together by devoted artists and monks. From the Ninth Century on, these scenes were prescribed and arranged according to an official scheme. The finest such collection still in existence is that of the 11th Century monastery church in Phocis, Greece, dedicated to Hosios Loukas, the holy hermit Luke. Its 150-odd mosaics comprise a textbook of the faith and a treasure house of Middle Byzantine art.

A MASTER PLAN FOR MOSAICS

It was Michael III, it is now believed, who established the official scheme of Byzantine church decoration when he built the Church of Our Lady of the Pharos at his palace in Constantinople. Thereafter worshipers, whether they could read or not, could lift up their eyes in any church in the empire and see all about them in precisely placed pictures the intricate theology of their faith.

The general outlines of this hierarchical scheme are indicated in the floor plan of Hosios Loukas below and the cutaway drawing of half the church at right. From the lower reaches of the church, representing the earthly world, mosaics of saints and martyrs, prophets and archangels rise in order of importance into Heaven, represented by the great dome, from which Christ as Lord of the Universe looks down. Scenes from Christ's life fill out the curved corners, or "squinches," below the dome and other areas in the church. The bema, or sanctuary, is covered by a smaller dome which shows the Twelve Apostles at the Pentecost, the founding of the Church on earth. From the vault of the apse, Mary, Mother of God, dominates the sanctuary—and the view of the worshipers.

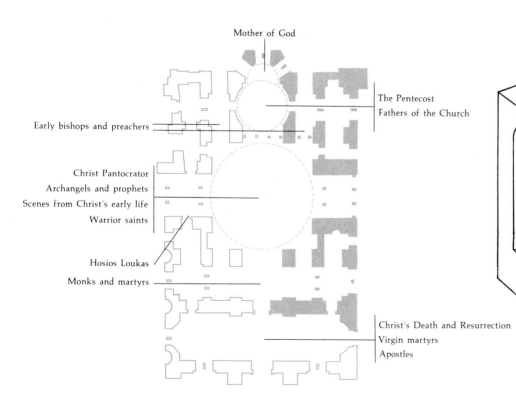

Mother of God

The Pentecost
Fathers of the Church

Early bishops and preachers

Christ Pantocrator
Archangels and prophets
Scenes from Christ's early life
Warrior saints

Hosios Loukas

Monks and martyrs

Small dome

Half-dome

APSE

BEMA

Christ's Death and Resurrection
Virgin martyrs
Apostles

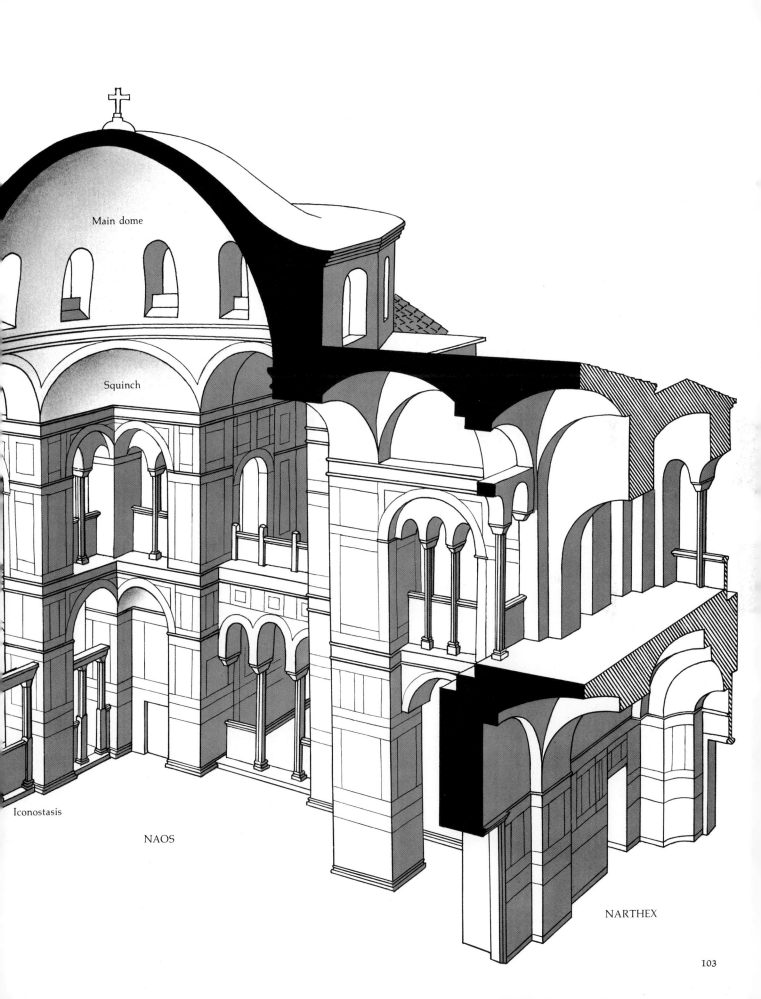

Main dome

Squinch

Iconostasis

NAOS

NARTHEX

In the entry, niches reveal the drama of death and resurrection

To the left of Hosios Loukas' main doorway is one of the church's key mosaics: the Crucifixion. In it Christ's eyes are closed; He is already dead. Seen mourning below the cross are His Mother, Mary, and St. John, His most beloved Apostle. Above the cross are the sun and moon with human faces.

In an act of love and humility on the eve of His agony, Jesus washes the feet of Peter as another Apostle unties a sandal. Ranged around the arch framing the niche are the Apostles Luke, Simon and Matthew; the two at the sides, as in many Byzantine church mosaics, are made narrow and elongated so they will shrink to proper proportions when seen from below.

THE NARTHEX contains what most art historians consider the finest mosaics in the church. The area is also located in gray on the plan above.

Aloof and austere, Christ as Lord of the Universe faces the narthex above the center doorway, with angels and the Virgin Mary above His head. He is calling attention to the Biblical passage in His left hand: "I am the light of the world; he that followeth Me shall not walk in darkness but shall have the light of life."

According to Christian doctrine, following Christ's death, He descended into Hell to free all the souls who had been lingering there since Adam's original sin. Above, King Solomon and King David (with beard) watch as Jesus leads Adam and Eve out of confinement. Below Christ's feet are the broken keys, locks and doors of Hell.

The niche at the right end of the narthex contains another scene of the Lord and His Apostles. Christ has pulled back His robes and at His bidding the doubtful Thomas, who had refused to believe that He had risen, is touching His wounds. On the arch above are figures of Thomas, Bartholomew and Philip.

Below the main dome of the church,
curved corner scenes portray the birth,
presentation and baptism of Christ

THE NAOS, *or main hall of the church, rises
to support the central dome, its square shape
converted into an octagon by arches crossing
each corner and forming small half-domes, or
squinches. In each of these concave surfaces,
mosaics depict early events in Christ's life.*

I*n one squinch Christ is shown being immersed by John the
Baptist in the waters of the Jordan while angels hold His
clothes. The Holy Spirit descends upon Jesus in the form of
a dove bearing an olive branch. The heavenly Hand pointing
at Him from above represents God the Father, who proclaims:
"Thou art My beloved Son; with Thee I am well pleased."*

A mosaic of the Nativity shows a haloed Mary busy caring for the newborn Jesus, who is singled out by the Star of Bethlehem, and is shown being bathed at right. A pensive Joseph sits at the left. Behind Joseph, the Magi, bearing gifts, approach in adoration while shepherds move in from the far right and angels hover in the sky.

In grave dignity—heightened by the curve of the squinch itself, which bends the figures reverently toward one another—Jesus is brought to the temple for presentation. On the right, Joseph bears the traditional offering of two pigeons. At left, Simeon, a high priest, prepares to take the Child from Mary as Anna, a prophetess, watches.

In the sanctuary, mosaics honor the Apostles and other holy
men and, above all, Mary, Mother of God

AN UPWARD VIEW *into the sanctuary's ceilin*
(right) shows the Apostles in the small dom
and the Virgin in the half-dome of the aps

T*he smaller of Hosios Loukas' two domes, located*
above the altar, depicts the Pentecost, the descent of
the Holy Spirit on the Apostles. They are assembled
in a circle, starting with the white-bearded Peter (cen-
ter right) and moving counterclockwise around to Paul
(center left). Tongues of fire are descending, giving
them the power to go forth and convert all nations.

O*n the half-dome covering the apse, the half-circle*
that terminates the sanctuary, Mary is enthroned both
as the Mother of God and Protectress of the Church.
Here she dominates the view of most worshipers, al-
though her position is theologically second to that of
Christ at the apex of the main dome. In her arms she
holds the Infant, whose hand is raised in blessing.

A medallion of St. Eleutherius (top), a Second Century Bishop of Rome, appears on the high wall to the right of the sanctuary. He is one of some 140 saints whose memories are evoked in the liturgy and whose portraits appear in the church. Below him is the wise Daniel, with hands raised above Darius' fierce lions who are turned miraculously tame. This subject was beloved of the Byzantine church decorators; Daniel's escape was believed to prefigure the resurrection of Christ.

THE ALMIGHTY FIGURE
IN THE DOME

At the center of the main dome of every Byzantine church, in the highest place of honor, is the figure of Christ as "Pantocrator," or Lord of the Universe. What the original Pantocrator in Hosios Loukas looked like, no one knows, for it was long ago destroyed. But the one in the Church of the Virgin at Daphni still exists and is shown here restored to its early brilliance. It ranks as the greatest portrait of its kind, and as one of the most powerful surviving works of Middle Byzantine art. Christ's piercing brown eyes—sad, remote, loving and severe—seem to look down into the very souls of the worshipers standing on the church floor below Him. Unhappily, the subtle achievement of the artist who created this exceptional figure cannot be discerned in other Byzantine mosaics still in existence. His masterpiece must remain, as a famous art historian has said, "lonely in its greatness and sacred austerity."

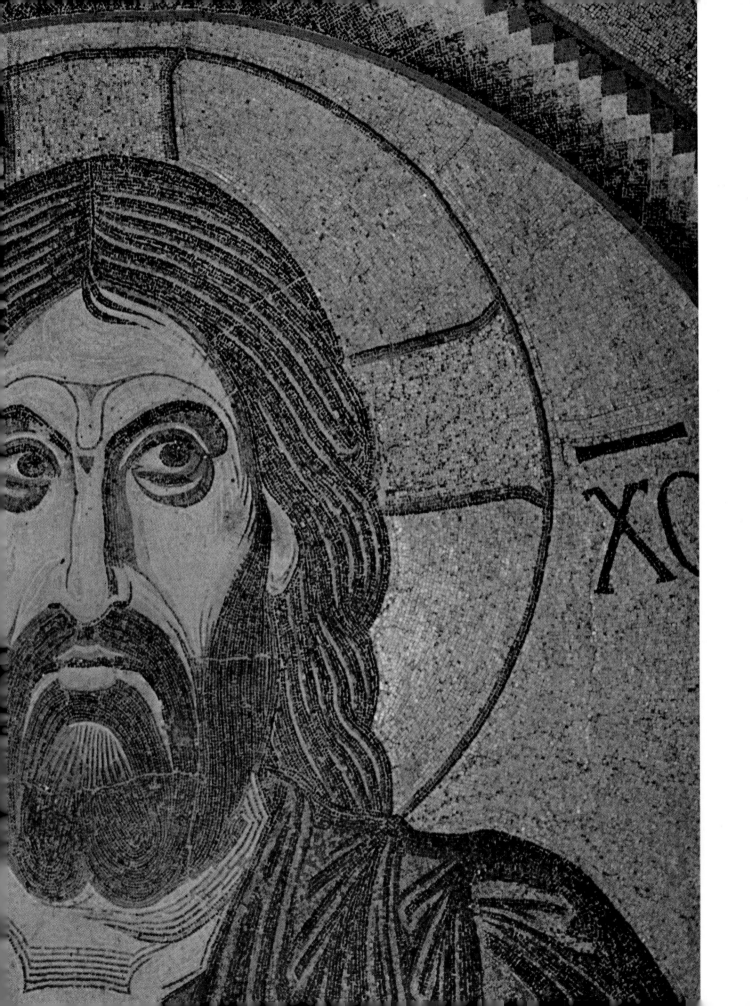

6

THE ROUND
OF BYZANTINE LIFE

Glimpses of the lives led by the men and women of Byzantium may still be obtained from various sources: accounts of the various saints, manuals of private and public law, historians' chronicles, secular and religious literature. In addition, something of the texture of Byzantine life still lurks in unexpected corners of the Greek world today—in monastery courtyards on Mount Athos, in the cobbled lanes of the small ruined hillside town of Mistra, on a spur of the Taygetus Mountains near the remains of ancient Sparta, in the color and lines of the caïques of remote Aegean fishing ports.

From the evidence we can extract information about an astonishing number of aspects of the daily life of the Byzantines and of the social and commercial structure of their society. We know a good deal about the amusements of the rich and poor alike, of their dress, of the place of women in Byzantine society. Moreover, we can follow changes that occurred in many of these things during the long life of the empire. We know the regulations that governed construction in Constantinople and we can appreciate the practical demonstration of the Byzantines' concern for the elderly and the sick among them. The elaborate commercial organization of the empire, which centered around the great city of Constantinople, is spelled out in considerable detail. We can piece together information about the circumstances of Byzantine life in the countryside regions, far from the commercial hub. Finally, we know that the religious belief around which the culture of Byzantium revolved was as shot through with superstition as a rich brocade is shot through with gold or silver fibers.

The life of the Byzantines was neither tedious nor uniform, as Edward Gibbon dourly described it. It abounded with opportunities for self-expression and independence. Even if the Byzantines were taught by their religion—and only too often had it confirmed in bitter experience—that humanity was exposed to endless tribulation and suffering, and that short of the Kingdom of Heaven man could expect little tranquillity or stability, this did not prevent them from making life an occasion for colorful pageantry or festive gaiety. They had an unfailing instinct for beauty, and it is inconceivable that this instinct did not affect their personal life,

DANCERS AND MUSICIANS *perform in this scene from an 11th Century illuminated manuscript. Their circular dance, musical instruments and headdress recall customs of ancient Greece, a major source of Byzantine culture.*

113

too, giving it something of the texture of a self-conscious work of art.

Preoccupied with religion and fate though they were, the Byzantines nevertheless found it easy to relax. Much of their social life was conducted out-of-doors. On every social level, friends and neighbors depended on each other for the pleasure of strolling and talking, often meeting in the streets and in the great open forums. Refreshments were available in cafés and restaurants; at some of these tables were moved outside in good weather, and facilities for games similar to dominoes and checkers were available. For those seeking to escape the congestion of Constantinople, there were pleasant walks along country roads extending beyond the city walls, gardens to stroll through near the water's edge, untouched woods and fields that could be reached by sailing a short distance from the city. Hunting was popular and the rich played a form of polo.

For those who preferred city life, distractions were provided almost daily by strolling musicians and itinerant jugglers. Public baths, like the pump rooms at the European spas so much in vogue in the 18th and 19th Centuries, also provided a setting for social gatherings. There were theaters for pantomimes, ballet and musical revues. Circuses and carnivals were held frequently, and jousting tournaments in the Western manner were sometimes staged.

The leading sport and the great focus of the life of the Byzantine masses was the chariot racing held at the Hippodrome. For these races a special bureaucracy developed, one that involved the most important citizen bodies of the empire, the *demes* (from *dêmos*, the people) or factions, as they have since been called. The factions, each of which supported its own entries in the races, had existed in Roman times, but at Byzantium they became so powerful that they had to be formed into organi-zations run somewhat on the lines of local militia. Although there were originally four factions—the Greens, Blues, Reds and Whites—the Greens and Blues later absorbed the other two.

Each of the surviving two factions had its own leader, or *demarch*. Beneath him there served a hierarchy of dignitaries and employees: treasurers, notaries, archivists, heralds, poets, musicians, organists, painters and sculptors, charioteers, circus performers (for the intervals between races), officials (to keep order in the Hippodrome), stablehands and others.

In addition to staging the chariot races in the Hippodrome, the factions performed other functions; they formed the emperor's escort in his cavalcades and in processions, they proclaimed the official acclamations or pieces of verse prepared for state occasions. They wore special clothes—cloaks and shoes of the barbarian Huns, tunics with wide billowing sleeves fastened tightly at the wrist—and their hair, cropped close in front, was allowed to grow long and hang down at the back. It was through them that popular feeling in Byzantium was given its main outlet, and unwise was the emperor who refused to listen to the people's voice as it was expressed by one or another of the factions, whether the question at issue was cheaper oil, fewer taxes, or the conduct of an unjust official.

On a racing day the whole city was tense and astir. Above the imperial box at the Hippodrome fluttered the emperor's standard. Crowds swarmed into the tiers of stone seats, and foreign ambassadors took the places reserved for them. In the seats closest to the arena, where fresh yellow sand was mingled with the pungent dust of cedar and strewn with flowers, sat the members of the factions with their colors: the Blues to the right of the imperial box, the Greens to the left. Finally, surrounded by generals and patricians, the emperor appeared. At a given signal, four doors beneath the royal box

A GOLD NECKLACE, *made up of decorative pendants and a cross on a chain of delicate leafy design, was one of the many exquisite pieces of jewelry worn by Byzantine women. The Byzantines also were known for their lavish costumes, which they decorated with precious stones and pearls.*

were opened, and four chariots, each drawn by four horses, dashed into the arena. To the thunder of hooves and the frantic cries of the factions, the races began.

They continued all during the morning and afternoon. After the fourth race came an interval. Clowns, acrobats or parades of exotic animals diverted the spectators as they ate their frugal meals —dried meat, salted fish, cooked beans, watermelons, lemons, oranges. Frequently hams, fruits and vegetables were distributed at the emperor's expense. After the interval, the races were resumed, and once more the roaring populace rocked in its seats as the sand flew beneath the horses' hooves.

In later centuries the power of the factions faded. But the Hippodrome itself remained in use until the capture of the city by the Latins in 1204, though by then it was feats of horsemanship more than chariot racing that drew the acclamations of the crowd. In the last years of the empire the stadium was left almost deserted, though young princes and scions of the noble houses still exercised their mounts there, or played polo.

In the Hippodrome, as elsewhere in Constantinople, the clothes worn by Byzantines revealed their place in society. By the time of Justinian the upper classes had discarded the Roman toga and replaced it with a long elaborate coat of brocade. Toward the end of the empire turbanlike headdresses and fur-trimmed peaked hats became fashionable. From the Seventh Century on, beards were common, shaving being considered a vulgar Western practice. Artisans and slaves wore a short-sleeved, knee-length tunic of undyed wool girdled at the waist and topped with a hood against the cold.

Women used a scarf as a headdress, winding it about the head, with the end falling to the shoulders. Over a tunic they wore a cloak with a hood that could completely conceal their heads. They also wore jewelry: bracelets of gold with repoussé decoration; necklaces of precious stones of gold or silver; gold earrings of intricate filigree work or shaped into a half-moon which was pierced into a pattern of animals or birds separated by a cross. Cosmetics were used. The one fault that Bertrandon de la Brocquière, a visitor to Constantinople early in the 15th Century, could find with the empress whom he watched leave Hagia Sophia was that she had painted her face, though "assuredly she had not any need of it."

The legal place of a woman in the social structure of Byzantium was a relatively favored one. Her dowry was safeguarded by a law that required her husband to settle on her sufficient property to equal the dowry's value. She could under certain circumstances control both her own and her husband's property, and with regard to her children's actions she enjoyed equal authority with her husband.

Woman's role in society varied according to her station. The empress, of course, had important opportunities for action and influence independent of the emperor; ladies of noble families had their own functions in imperial ceremonies corresponding to those of their male counterparts. Lower down the social scale women raised their families, succored the poor, and often worried about their souls. Theoctista, mother of the famous Abbot Theodore, of the monastery of Stoudion, was a notable example. She was abstinent and charitable, sharing her board with the poor and the outcast. On feast days she gave her servants richer food—fish, fresh meat, chicken and better wine—instead of the usual bread, bacon and cheap wine. Occasionally she would beat her servants, but then she would fall on her knees before them, imploring their pardon. In the end she persuaded herself, her husband, her three brothers-in-law and her children to abandon everything and devote themselves to God.

Theodota, mother of the historian Michael Psellus, was a more serene, less austere character. Happy in her marriage to a handsome husband, she devoted herself to Psellus' education. She too received the poor at her table, serving them herself and washing their feet. After Psellus' sister died, Theodota was so overwhelmed with grief that she retired to a convent. There, after a short novitiate in which she weakened herself by abstaining from even the barest necessities of life, she died.

The charitable activities of generous women like Theoctista and Theodota were, of course, overshadowed by the philanthropy practiced by the church and prominent citizens. The records show that construction of hospitals and homes for the aged or infirm was a frequent assignment for the builders and architects of Byzantium. The hospital of the monastery of St. Savior Pantocrator, endowed by John II Comnenus in the 12th Century, contained 50 beds divided into five wards, with separate wards for surgical cases, for medical cases and for women. It was attended by ten male doctors and one female doctor, with a supplementary staff of male and female assistants, special inspectors of the mainly vegetarian food, a herbalist and a professor of medicine for the instruction of new doctors. Many records survive of endowments made specifically for the support of institutions of this sort.

While charitable work was largely the province of private benefactors or the Church, much of the everyday life of the healthy and provident was organized by a system of guilds, administered by public officials. A handbook issued about 900 A.D., known as "The Book of the Prefect," gives details of the system. It opens with a preface by the emperor: "Having created all things and made order and harmony reign in the world, God engraved the Law with His own finger on the Tables, and set it forth for all to see so that it might prevent by a

A NOMISMA, *or bezant, bears the portrait of Constantine VII Porphyrogenitus. So stable was the value of this gold coin that it became a medium of exchange from Western Europe to Central Asia, and was used in such remote lands as Russia and India.*

happy discipline the members of the human family from hurling themselves one upon the other and the stronger from crushing the weaker. . . . It is for this reason that it has appeared good to our Serenity also to formulate the dispositions which result from the Law, so that the human race is governed as is fitting and so that one person does not oppress another."

Every industry had its own guild. Some 21 major guilds—some with subguilds—controlled the life of all the artisans and tradesmen. No man could belong to two. Son generally succeeded father in the same trade. It was the prefect, or *eparch*, of the city who, among other functions, administered the system of guilds: though each guild could appoint its own president, the appointment probably had to be endorsed by the prefect. In fact, all the affairs of the guilds were virtually dependent on the prefect. Combining in his office the roles of chief justice, chief of police and regulator of the city's commercial and human traffic, the prefect was the most important functionary in the city—except for the emperor, who nominated him and could at any moment dismiss him.

Any infringement of guild regulations was punished by expulsion, and this meant compulsory retirement. Each member of a guild had to practice only his own trade: the goldsmith could deal only with gold, the candlemakers with candles, soapmakers with soap. Wages and hours were regulated. The guildsman owned his own capital, tools, raw materials and the articles he fabricated. There were no middlemen, for each guildsman offered his product directly to the consumer. Each guild could carry on its trade only in the particular quarter of the city

allocated to it, though grocers, with their more perishable goods, were allowed to have a shop anywhere. Various unpaid public services, including police work, also were required of the guilds.

The state levied 10 per cent on all imports and exports and imposed other taxes on consumer goods, inheritances, land and serf households. The state also had its own enterprises. The best silk came from the imperial factory, and certain dyes were reserved for use in the imperial household.

It was in the law, perhaps, that the state had its greatest impact on the lives of most people. The body of law revised by Justinian was more Roman than Christian in spirit: despite the opposition of the Church, divorce and slavery were both retained; at the same time wives, children and slaves now had more rights. Most cases were settled in lower courts in Constantinople and the provinces, but the more important suits could be taken to a high court of 12 judges, or to the emperor himself, who was the ultimate judge of appeals. In criminal cases the punishments were fines, the confiscation of property, death, or the loss of an eye or a hand. After the Eighth Century the death penalty was reserved for murder, treason and desertion and was used less and less often. Some murderers were even spared on the condition that they become monks and turn over half their property to their victim's heirs.

In his control of all aspects of Byzantine public and commercial life, the emperor also undertook public works—the building of palaces, fortifications, aqueducts, roads, as well as the manufacture of armaments.

The building regulations in Constantinople were strict, though it is impossible to know how stringently they were applied. Streets had to be 12 feet wide. Balconies on private houses had to be 15 feet above the ground and were not to extend to within 10 feet of the opposite wall. Owners of private houses with an unobstructed view of the sea (or of gardens or public monuments) had a right to protect that view—though it was stipulated that if anyone claimed a direct view of a monument of historical significance, such as a statue of Achilles or Ajax, he had to prove that he had enough education to appreciate it.

The state alone minted the gold coinage, whose principal unit was a coin containing some 65 grains of gold. This coin was known in Byzantium as the *nomisma*, elsewhere as the *bezant*. For seven centuries, from the reign of Constantine I to that of Nicephorus III Botaniatus, the bezant retained its value. It was a handsome, brilliant coin; one Byzantine merchant, trying to convince the King of Ceylon that the Byzantine monarch was a greater man than the King of Persia, successfully used the impressive bezant as a clincher. In the Eighth Century, when the Venerable Bede, the great English historian, wished to praise a British princess, he described her as being "pure as a bezant." It was not until the 11th Century that the coinage began to lose its universal respect and trust.

The empire's complex commercial life was centered in Constantinople. Strategically located astride the main routes between Europe and Asia, it was unusually well situated for such a role. From all points of the compass came the caravans and fleets to pour their merchandise into the customs houses, depots and workshops of the capital. Although many of these goods were passed on to the West, a large percentage remained to provide the raw materials for the capital's own workshops, where they were converted into finished articles either for home consumption or for re-export. Other cities and districts also had their workshops. By the 11th Century Thebes and Corinth, for instance, had their own silk industries, and carpets were manufactured in the Peloponnese.

For the Byzantine peasant and the small land-owner life must have been much as it is for the Turkish or Balkan peasant today—or at least as it was before the introduction of mechanical agricultural implements. But the life of the landed proprietor, particularly in Anatolia, where large estates developed from the Ninth Century onward, must have been one of considerable affluence and luxury. As early as the Eighth Century one agriculturist—and he was not the wealthiest—could give a dinner party for 36 guests, who were seated around a table of ivory and gold. This same land-owner could count among his stock 12,000 head of sheep, 800 oxen and 900 horses and mules, as well as a large number of serfs.

Since the entire life of all Byzantines—artisan, aristocrat, goldsmith, seaman, general, mother of a family—was dominated by religion, the atmosphere was impregnated with a sense of the supernatural. Often this deteriorated into arrant superstition. Byzantium was seldom free from the threat of invasion; with the specter of doom never far off it is hardly surprising that nervous tensions were generated. These expressed themselves at some times in what appears to have been wanton cruelty, and at others in recourse to astrology and necromancy, divination and black magic. Dreams and visions, the Byzantines believed, foretold events to come. Inanimate objects might have some crucial influence on a person's life or even on the fate of the empire. Books on the significance of numbers or on the meanings of thunder or earthquakes or the lunar phases, were widely read. Mediums plied their trade, though probably not to any greater extent than they do in many places today.

Constantinople itself was believed to be full of omens, concealed in mysterious inscriptions or obscure bas-reliefs carved on statues or columns. Could these have been deciphered, in fact, they might have predicted for the inhabitants the terrifying last days of their city.

A DEVOUT CHURCHGOER, *wearing a cowl like her Byzantine forebears, returns from Palm Sunday services.*

ISLAND OF THE PAST

In the heartland of Byzantium, villages still exist where life goes on almost exactly as it did under the empire. In the Greek island community of Olympos, windmills still grind grain to flour, housewives still bake bread in outdoor ovens, cobblers still make shoes by hand. Olympos has not been entirely passed over by the 20th Century: its men wear factory-made clothes, for example, and gas burners are in use. But in agriculture and religion, in customs and outlook, the people of Olympos are scarcely different from those who lived there a thousand years ago.

THE IMPERIAL EAGLE, *which appears in old Byzantine illuminations such as the one pictured at right, can still be seen decorating the buildings of Olympos (far right). The two-headed bird was adopted as an emblem by the Palaeologus family, the last Byzantine dynasty, to symbolize an empire that looked both West and East.*

ECHOES OF EMPIRE
IN A RURAL OUTPOST

Olympos, clinging to a mountainside on the island of Karpathos between Crete and Rhodes, is probably the most isolated community in Greece. The electric lights in the church and the airplanes that occasionally fly overhead would have astounded the Byzantines, but most modern conveniences have not reached the village. For example, there is only one telephone in town, and the mailman arrives from the town of Pigadia (pop. 1,000) only once a week (he must travel on foot since no roads connect the two communities). Such isolation has kept Olympos much as it was when it was first built on its present site in the Ninth Century A.D.

As in Byzantine days, some houses are still made of sun-dried bricks and roofed with wooden beams covered with straw, dirt and grass; the one large room of each house still contains a raised platform, called a "sofa," and a small family altar. Outside are a courtyard, a barn and a kitchen wing where the meals are prepared. Food is either grown by the family or bartered; many goods in Olympos are exchanged, rather than bought, since there is little currency in the village.

The villagers supplement their meager diet by hunting wild birds, a favorite sport during the empire, and by fishing. Before they set sail the men mend the nets they have woven and the fish traps they have fashioned out of split cane and twine. The Byzantines prepared for the day at sea in exactly the same way, and they offered up, in the early morning hours, the identical prayers for safety to the local protector of fishermen, St. Nicholas.

A MOUNTAIN VILLAGE of *whitewashed buildings and terraced farms, Olympos overlooks the Aegean. The village, originally built on the shore, was moved up after repeated pirate raids.*

WINDING YARN, *a woman of Olympos—like the Byzantine woman in the 13th Century miniature shown above her—holds a crude spindle onto which tufts of wool have been drawn and twisted into strands.*

TENDING THE CROPS, *a farm woman strides through fields below the town. Her scarflike headdress dates back to the Byzantine period, as does the mattock she carries for turning the rocky soil.*

TIMELESS TASKS OF HOME AND FARM

Farmers were for centuries the backbone of the Byzantine empire, and they are still the main support of local village economies. In former times the crops and livestock they raised fed not only their families but also provided for the aristocracy and hundreds of monastic establishments. The heavy taxes they paid financed the large standing armies that guarded Byzantium's frontiers and supported the glittering extravagance of the emperor's court.

Most of these burdens have long since been lifted, but the farmers of Olympos still labor at the same tasks. When women are not doing domestic chores—baking in communal ovens, embroidering, weaving cloth on hand looms—they toil in the fields beside their husbands. In hilly Olympos, where plows cannot be used, the villagers must do all their farming by hand, relying on the simple tools of their ancestors—hoes, mattocks, sickles and scythes.

ORNATE BREAD *for Easter is made with swirling designs around an egg. As in Byzantine times, the bread is eaten during the Easter Sunday meal, whi*

PREPARING FOR EASTER

The similarities between imperial and present-day Olympos are never more marked than during the Easter season. Just as their ancestors did, the women bake ceremonial loaves of bread decorated with traditional designs. The day before Eas-

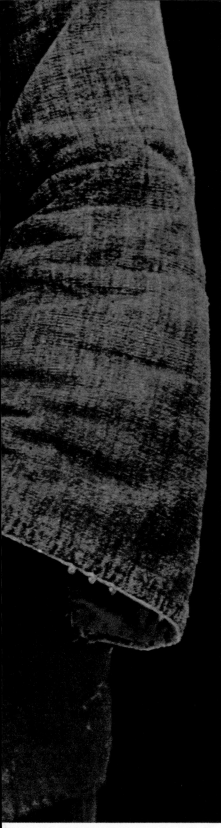

so includes stuffed goat, thick cream and wine.   COLORING EGGS, *housewives dye many of them red to recall the blood Christ shed on the Cross.*

ter each family kills a lamb or young goat, the first meat it will eat after the Lenten fast ends on Sunday. The woman of the house displays her prized possessions, such as heirloom dishes and woven bedspreads, and puts flowers around the family altar. She and her husband also scrub their house from floor to roof and whitewash the walls inside and out. Finally, early on Easter day, they welcome in their neighbors, who come to exchange gifts, kisses and wishes for a happy holiday.

125

IN SOLEMN CONVOCATION, *worshipers surround the Crucifix on Good Friday. To commemorate the death of Christ, the priest has removed the cross from the altar and has placed it in the center of the church.*

ICONS OF SAINTS, *wrapped in brig cloths, are carried from the church the village cemetery for services hon ing the dead. The devout pay for t privilege of carrying the icons up ea step on the way back to the chur*

BOY CHORISTERS *sing hymns of joy dur ing the "Christ is Risen" service held at midnight to mark the beginning of Easter. The young singers start to learn simplified Byzantine musical nota tions when they are only six or seven.*

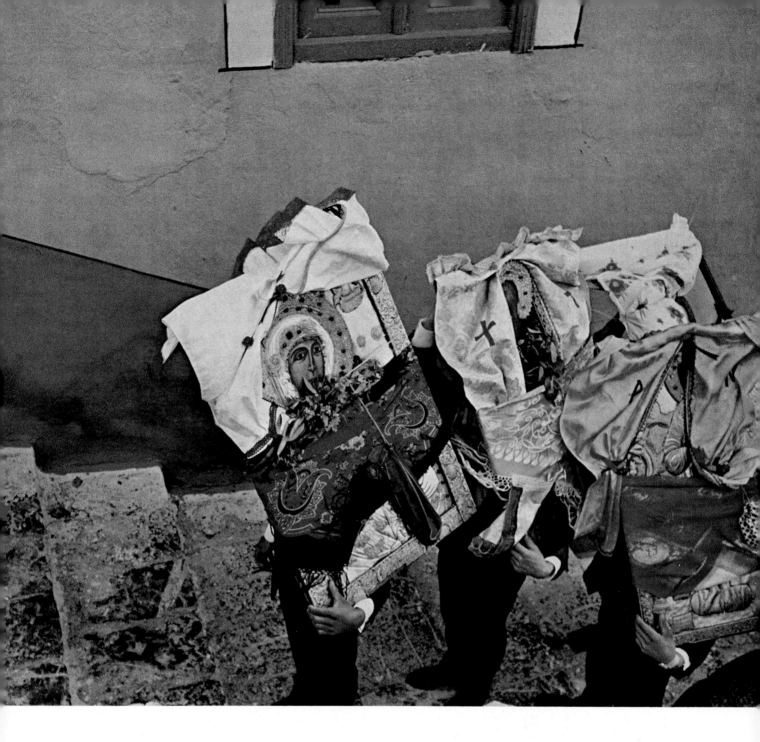

THE PAGEANTRY OF HOLY WEEK

On Good Friday the villagers mourn the death of Christ and on Saturday night they celebrate His Resurrection. The congregation gathers in church near midnight in total darkness; as Easter Sunday begins, the priest lights candles held by the faithful. On the next Tuesday, the people of Olympos carry icons to the cemetery. Like the farmers of Byzantium, they believe the icons can ward off drought. Thus, in addition to regular religious services at the graves, the priest says prayers for rain. The congregation's deep personal involvement during Holy Week recalls the lines of a Byzantine poet: "Yesterday, Christ, I was buried together with you! With you arising, I arise."

127

AN IMPERIAL COUPLE, *Romanus and Eudoxia, are crowned by Christ in a carved ivory relief that dates from the 10th Century.*

A TRADITIONAL WEDDING

Because the Church forbids weddings during Lent, a great many take place just after Easter. Marriages are still arranged by the parents—almost always within the village. On the long-awaited day, the groom comes with a band of musicians to the bride's home, following an ancient Greek custom handed down by the Byzantines. During the ceremony the priest leads the couple and their bridal party three times around the altar as well-wishers chant songs, throw rice and slap the groom on the back.

A VILLAGE COUPLE *receives a blessing as they are united in marriage. Their crowns of paper and flowers, traditional since Byzantine times, are joined by a ribbon signifying the bonds of matrimony.*

129

ON A HOMEMADE BAGPIPE, *fashioned from goatskin, a musician plays for the dancers.*

IN AN ANCIENT DANCE, *villagers move in a circle during a banque*

AN OLD-STYLE BANQUET

Festivals and banquets have been a favorite diversion of Greeks since ancient times. During the empire they gave up the classical habit of reclining on couches, and the Church insisted that the sexes sit at separate tables. It is in this same fashion that feasts and spirited dances are now held in Olym-

...ld in the church square of Olympos on the town's memorial day. Men sit together at tables; to eat in public with their wives would violate tradition.

pos as the climax to weddings or religious holidays. If the banquet occurs on a memorial day, as is the case with the one shown here, the people eat food which they have placed that morning as an offering on the graves of their dead. One such food eaten on memorial occasions is *kolyva*, a mixture of wheat, nuts and fruit which the Byzantine Christians adopted from the pagan Greeks in the Fourth Century. Only men may play the musical instruments; they also take turns improvising lyrics for songs to suit the occasion—exactly as the Byzantines used to invent verses at feasts and festivals.

131

A WAYSIDE CHAPEL *on the edge of the village, like a score of other small private chapels in Olympos, was built by a pious townsman in gratitude fo*

e help of a saint to whom he had appealed. In Byzantine times peasants often built such chapels on their property and rededicated their lives to God.

7

A GLITTERING CULTURE

Through nearly eleven centuries, the splendor of Byzantine achievements in literature and the arts reflected not only the dominance of the Christian Church, but also the intellectual and artistic tastes of the empire's aristocracy which supported it. The upper level of Byzantium's society was not simply the possessor of power and prestige; it was also a highly cultivated class, with an almost passionate regard for learning and a sensitive eye for beauty.

In education and literature the Byzantines zealously cherished their Greco-Roman heritage, studying and preserving for posterity the great writings of the classical past and adding to them notable contributions of their own. And in ecclesiastical architecture and works of art—frescoes and brilliant mosaics, exquisite carvings in ivory, illuminated manuscripts—the culture of the Byzantines found its fullest, most original expression.

A good education, in Byzantium, was considered one of the major virtues, and a must for anyone ambitious to better himself. To be uneducated was a disgrace. Added to the religious distinction between a Christian Byzantine and a barbarian was an essential feeling of superiority: the Byzantine believed he was an educated man, and was convinced that all barbarians were ignorant.

The principal requirement of this education was a knowledge of classical culture—the speech and literature of the ancient Hellenic world. There was no break with the tradition of Greco-Roman pagan civilization, even among those who were to become the great masters of theology of the Christian Church.

Through most of Byzantine history the course of studies remained more or less constant, though many changes took place in educational institutions. Foremost among the disciplines was grammar, that is, the correct use of classical Greek. Until the time of Justinian, students were taught the use of both Latin and Greek, but by then Latin as the language of the state was dying out. By the middle of the Seventh Century Greek had completely taken over. But Byzantium—like the modern Greek state, where divergence in language is still a living issue—had its linguistic problems. Besides the constantly evolving vernacular Greek

PRESERVING THE PAST, *two monks restore manuscripts in an abbey near Padua in Italy. Hanging behind them are pages from Geronticum Quodam, a 13th Century Byzantine tract on the lives of the apostles and saints.*

spoken by the Byzantine populace and based on the *koine* or common tongue of Hellenistic times, there was "Atticized" Greek, a consciously purified form akin to the classical Greek of Thucydides and Demosthenes. This was the spoken and written language of the court and of the cultured upper class, and provided a model to which the formal secular literature adhered.

Included in grammar was the study of classical literature. This demanded an intimate acquaintance with all the major classical authors, particularly with Homer. After the Bible, Homer's *Iliad* and *Odyssey* were by far the best known and most frequently quoted works. The story is told of an 11th Century emperor who defied convention by having his beautiful mistress take part in the imperial procession. Shocked by this breach of propriety, the spectators were placated by hearing a courtier quote from the *Iliad* the passage in which the old men of Troy gaze at Helen passing by and murmur:

Nor Greeks nor Trojans one can rightly blame
That, for a woman's sake so beautiful
They have alike endured so many woes.

Great centers of learning were liberally distributed throughout the empire. Many of the schools famous in pagan times, including those at Alexandria, Antioch, Beirut and Athens, continued to flourish until well into the Christian era. In addition, Constantine the Great encouraged education by founding a school at his new capital, and in 425 Theodosius II opened the university at Constantinople. Staffing the university were five Greek and three Latin sophists or rhetoricians, 10 Greek and 10 Latin grammarians, two jurists and a philosopher. Between the Seventh and Ninth Centuries, however, Byzantine learning endured a dark period: the university at Athens had already been closed by Justinian in 529 and now the schools at Alexandria, Antioch and Beirut passed into Moslem hands. Even the university at Constantinople seems to have suffered an eclipse. Nevertheless, opportunities for higher learning were never entirely absent, and private teachers were always to be found for those who could afford them.

In the 11th Century, the university at Constantinople was revived and reorganized, and several new schools were established there. Learning was again widespread, although it was to know another dim period following the sack of Constantinople by the Crusaders in 1204. The 14th and 15th Centuries saw a final flowering of learning. It was then, even as the Christian empire of Byzantium was slowly but surely succumbing, that the Byzantines looked back on their pagan heritage with special pride. This was the time when many Byzantine intellectuals began to call themselves "Hellenes" and not "Romaioi" (Romans), as they had in the past.

As a result of the continual emphasis on the classics, much secular literature of the Byzantines tended to imitate these ancient models. Yet in certain fields Byzantine secular writers produced original works of great merit. One of the fields was poetry. Many short poems in Atticized Greek have survived; epigrammatic in style, they are marked by wit and a sensitive imagery reminiscent of the Cavalier poets of 17th Century England.

In the category of popular romances, which were written in a more vernacular language, Byzantium has to its credit one of the most magnificent of all epic poems, *Digenes Akrites*. This 11th Century work, which has come down in several versions, has been compared in quality to the *Song of Roland*. It is a dramatic tale of the eastern border-districts of the empire (Akrites means "borderer" in Greek), of a frontier far from the sophisticated, formal atmosphere of the Byzantine court. Here, where fighting between Moslems and Christians was sporadic and warfare against robber bands was constant, a landowning, militaristic aristocracy had emerged. This self-assertive and strongly individualistic world provides the stage for the heroic exploits in love and war of the border lord Digenes. Included among his deeds are his courtship and kidnaping of the lovely Eudoxia, his battles with wild beasts and his merciless warfare against brigands.

Digenes, son of a Moslem father and a Christian mother, appears as the ideal of chivalry—handsome, fair, broad-chested, clad in a red tunic embroidered with pearls and fastened with golden buttons. The bridle of his white horse is enameled gold, its saddle cloth adorned with turquoise. Digenes' wife brings him a splendid dowry, and his house is paneled with gold and mosaics. After a long and adventurous life, the warrior-hero becomes ill, and as he dies, his wife Eudoxia, unable to bear the separation, falls lifeless beside him.

History was another secular field enriched by the Byzantines. Many of their historians wrote works of judgment, scope and critical maturity. Procopius in the Sixth Century, for example, vigorously recounted the wars of Justinian. In the 11th Century Michael Psellus wrote a celebrated history of that age, and Anna Comnena—perhaps the greatest of women historians—described the reign of her father, Emperor Alexius I. The memoirs of John VI Cantacuzene, written after his abdication as emperor in 1354, are a valuable source for the troubled history of the Balkan regions in the 14th Century.

While Byzantine secular literature sometimes reached heights of distinction and originality, it was generally surpassed in quality by religious literature, both prose and verse. St. Basil, St. John Chrysostom, St. Gregory of Nyssa, St. Gregory of Nazianzus, St. Maximus the Confessor—these are but a few of the writers of lucid and profound theological prose who have few equals among Christian authors.

SINGING BY SYMBOLS

Byzantine hymns were composed according to a system of signs, as illustrated in a famous 12th Century manuscript (below). These signs, drawn above the Greek words, give the intervals, rhythms and accents to follow from a starting note—in this case the modern note "a"—determined by a "signature" preceding the hymn (light gray figures at upper right of manuscript). The symbols, or neumes, are shown with modern transcription; some are translated at bottom.

MANUSCRIPT

TRANSCRIPTION

Κύ-ρι-ε, ἡ ἐν πολ-λαῖς ἁ-μαρ-τί-
Lord, the woman

αις πε-ρι-πε-σοῦ σα γυ-νὴ
fallen in many sins,

INTERVALS	INTERVALS WITH ACCENTS	RHYTHMS
repeated note		
ascending second (a to b)	ascending second with staccato	note value doubled
descending second (a to g)		
descending third (a to f)	ascending second with stress	note value prolonged by half

The poetical hymns of Byzantium are also virtually unmatched in Christian literature, and some rank with the great literary treasures of the Western world. They combine lyrical beauty with dramatic and human intensity, often expressed in an animated dialogue that recalls the drama of the ancient Greeks or the medieval miracle plays of Western Europe. Among the outstanding hymnodists were Romanus the Melode, a Sixth Century deacon considered the greatest poet of the Byzantines; St. John of Damascus, who in the Eighth Century created some of the finest hymns of the Byzantine Christian Church; Casia, a Ninth Century beauty who forfeited a chance to become empress and devoted her life as a nun to composing religious poems, and St. Simeon the New Theologian, a Constantinopolitan of the early 11th Century who wrote fervent mystical odes.

Not only in literature and music but in architecture, too, Byzantium's achievements in the religious field outshone its creations for secular use. Very little secular architecture of the Byzantine empire survives; such buildings as palaces, villas and public baths are known mainly through archeological excavations and, in general, do not seem to have been unusual in their designs. A number of utilitarian structures remain, among them city walls and cisterns of ingenious construction, but like the Roman aqueducts they are more triumphs of engineering skill than of architectural design. Thus our understanding of Byzantine architecture rests almost exclusively on church buildings, many of which fortunately still stand.

Soon after the empire was founded, its architects launched themselves on a highly inventive course, and before very long they had established a distinctive ecclesiastical style that changed but little over a millennium. The roots of the style lay in the Fourth and Fifth Century architecture of Pergamum, Ephesus, Miletus and other Greek cities near the Aegean coast of Anatolia. From those centuries and that region sprang the basic architectural elements of the Byzantine church—multiple vaulting, the dome and the centralized plan.

Centralized planning was derived in part from the centralized form of Greek and Roman tombs. But it was brought about more directly by the custom, common in Fifth Century Greek basilicas (which were oblong churches), of having the Mass performed in the whole central nave of the church instead of at one end, while the faithful stood in the aisles along three sides. But the long, rectangular plan of the basilica was inappropriate for a service that occupied only the central area of the church, and Byzantine church builders gradually adopted a more compact and suitable scheme, one that usually took the shape of a Greek cross.

Vaulting, the technique of constructing curved ceilings of masonry, was borrowed from the secular architecture of the Greek coastal cities, where it was frequently used in palaces and in public buildings, but almost never in churches. However, the idea of a crowning dome, which is a particular kind of vault, seems to have had its origin in the widespread use of domes over the tombs of early Christian martyrs, and in the domed buildings of Rome and Persia. It is a tribute to the genius of Byzantine architects that they successfully brought together these devices—the centralized plan, the vault and the dome—as the key elements of a wholly new architectural style.

Byzantium's architecture, like its other arts, falls into three recognizable periods—Early, Middle and Late—each distinct in its characteristics. The Early Byzantine period, from the early Sixth to the mid-Ninth Centuries, was an age of lively experiment in building design and the time in which a standard centralized church type was first established. The finest churches of the era are from the

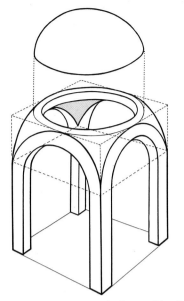

THE PENDENTIVE *was one device used by Byzantine architects to erect a round dome on the square central area of a church. In effect they put a hemisphere on a square box and cut away the hemisphere's crown and overlapping sides. This left four spherical triangles (see shaded area in sketch), on which a smaller dome or hemisphere could rise.*

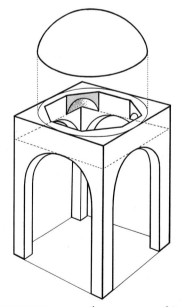

THE SQUINCH *was another common architectural device used to dome the square. Its function was to convert the square into an octagon by building up each corner with a series of overlapping masonry arches laid across the angle of the square. The resulting form was sufficiently close to a circle to accommodate the round base of the dome.*

reign of Justinian, and the monumental Hagia Sophia, built between 532 and 537 in Constantinople, is not only the biggest but also one of the finest examples. Clear in its basic outline, it is complex and sophisticated in its parts. Its unique plan, its enormous size, the extraordinary richness of its carved marble—these are among the features that make Hagia Sophia the crowning glory of Byzantine architecture. But at the same time its very uniqueness separates Hagia Sophia from the mainstream of architectural development.

Typically, the standard Early Byzantine church was small. The core of the building was cross-shaped. Thick piers supported a dome over the intersection of the arms of the cross; barrel vaults spanned each of the four arms. Additional vaulted areas, set in the angles formed by the arms of the cross, gave the building a rectangular plan. Though the church itself was small, the effect within was one of spaciousness and clarity; this was due partly to the simplicity of the piers and arches and partly to bright, steady light streaming through large windows set in the dome and walls. The church's exterior was plain yet impressive, composed of only a few simple geometric shapes and pierced by single-arched, unadorned windows.

This domed-cross type of church spread to Greece and through most of Anatolia. More distant parts of the empire, however, retained much of their earlier styles of church design or developed new styles of their own which were largely independent of Early Byzantine architecture. Thus Sixth and Seventh Century churches in Mesopotamia and Egypt differed but little from Fourth and Fifth Century examples in those areas; in plan they were oblong basilicas, and domes were rarely, if ever, used. In Bulgaria and Armenia, on the other hand, far more sophisticated styles emerged, suffused with a richness of architectural effects not found in typical Early Byzantine churches. These styles depended to some extent on the basilica plan, but they also were often based on circular or octagonal plans.

During the Middle Byzantine era (late Ninth to mid-13th Centuries) there was no longer a single basic church type. Now four different centralized types prevailed, each consisting of a domed core made up of various combinations of the cross, the octagon and the square. Almost all of these churches were very small. The most common type, called the cross-in-square, probably evolved from the Early Byzantine domed-cross church, which it resembled in plan. In the cross-in-square church, however, the vaulted areas in the angles of the cross arms were visually united to the cruciform core by sharply reducing the size of the dome-supporting piers. In many cases the piers simply became columns. This visual link between the cross-shaped core and the four-corner bays made the church appear broader, and gave it an intricacy and subtlety lacking in Early Byzantine structures.

In other ways, too, the simplicity and clarity of the earlier churches had vanished. Where formerly a window-opening was spanned by a single arch, it was now generally divided into two or three arches. Windows grew fewer and smaller, and as a result the interiors of the churches became obscure, seemingly bathed in twilight. In addition, every surface of these small Middle Byzantine buildings was finely wrought. A wealth of carved stone details ornamented their interiors; on the exteriors bricks were frequently set in decorative patterns and a series of moldings framed doors and windows and ran along cornice lines. The buildings' profiles became more complex—the dome now rested upon a high cylindrical drum, there was a variety of roof levels, and brick buttresses and half-columns projected from the body of the church.

A number of distinctly different local architectural schools flourished throughout the empire during the Middle Byzantine period. In Cappadocia in east-central Anatolia, for instance, tiny churches were carved out of living rock, faithfully copying larger free-standing buildings. In Greece the exteriors of churches were lavishly adorned with intricately patterned brickwork. Middle Byzantine architecture in Italy, on the other hand, was mostly crude and provincial, often heavily modified by Western architectural traditions. The exception is St. Mark's in Venice; St. Mark's, however, is not so much a Middle Byzantine church as it is an 11th Century copy of a Sixth Century original—the Church of the Holy Apostles in Constantinople, built by Justinian on the site of Constantine's church of the same name.

The four basic church types of the Middle Byzantine era, as well as most of their stylistic features, continued into the Late Byzantine period, which lasted until the fall of Constantinople in 1453. But there were differences. Architects of the Late Byzantine period stressed verticality, both inside and out, and they achieved this effect as much by the increased use of such vertical elements as columns, piers and buttresses as by the actual heightening of the buildings. Middle Byzantine churches usually had but one dome; those of the Late period often had five—a large dome over the center and a smaller one over each corner.

Although Constantinople remained relatively faithful to the principle of subordinating surface patterns to overall design, Late Byzantine churches elsewhere displayed exterior surfaces of unprecedented richness; intricate brickwork was more widely used than ever before and moldings, blind arches and other decorative devices abounded. Even the rims of domes became scalloped as they followed the curves of arched windows piercing their drums. But seldom were the resulting effects of these embellishments of the same high quality that had marked Byzantine architecture during its earlier great eras.

Notable as Byzantium's contributions to architecture were, it is the empire's magnificent heritage of other arts for which it is chiefly remembered. As in architecture—and in literature, music and in all other aspects of Byzantine culture—it was the Church that provided the principal focus for the creativity of the era's artists, who glorified church interiors with mosaics and frescoes and beautified objects for religious use. In addition, their talent displayed itself in secular art of an elegance unsurpassed in the medieval world.

The art of the Byzantine empire, while primarily the art of the Church, was also the art of Constantinople. The capital's great artistic importance was based on the fact that nearly all the wealthy and educated patrons of the arts resided there: the city was the seat of the emperor and his court; the aristocracy and the rich merchants made it their home; the monastic orders and the patriarchate were headquartered there. Though the empire itself slowly shrank in size, the stability and continuity of cultural life in the capital went on undiminished, century after century.

This enormous concentration of power and wealth in one city affected Byzantine art in several fundamental ways. First, Constantinople's continuity of culture in general nourished the growth of a strong artistic tradition. A 12th Century artist in Constantinople, for example, was never far from his artistic past; he was constantly surrounded by works of earlier Byzantine artists. Undoubtedly he tried to emulate their greatness, and in so doing he naturally looked deeply into their forms and learned from what he saw.

Second, art radiated out from the capital in veritable streams. Illuminated manuscripts, icons, ivories and metalwork were exported from Constantinople to every quarter of the empire and even far beyond its borders. The city's artists themselves were summoned to the imperial provinces and to neighboring countries to execute murals for administrators, princes and churchmen. In the early Eighth Century, when the Moslem rulers of Syria wanted to decorate their Great Mosque at Damascus, they sent to Constantinople for mosaicists to help them. The art produced in Constantinople established the standards for Byzantine taste throughout the empire; local artists in the outlying areas fashioned their work according to artistic developments in the capital.

In all these arts, a distinctively Byzantine style did not emerge until about the Sixth Century, having evolved from mixed origins. Its principal antecedent was early Christian art. In the beginning, in the Second and Third Centuries, this art was mainly that of the catacombs at Rome. It was almost exclusively tomb art—frescoes and sarcophagi. Its style, if generally cruder, differed little from contemporary pagan works. The figures—Christ as a shepherd, for example—were naturalistic; they had depth and freedom of movement and attention was given to facial features and the play of muscles.

In the early Fourth Century, after the toleration of Christianity had been decreed, this art came out of the catacombs. Christians began to build churches in great numbers and to decorate their interiors. The art they produced continued to draw upon the classical style of pagan Rome. But the Christians now began to modify classicism and gradually created another style of their own.

Particularly important to the growth of this new style was Roman imperial portraiture of the late Third and early Fourth Centuries, which demanded an impersonal, almost symbolic representation accenting the emperor's divine majesty rather than his true likeness. From this the Christians adopted for their own revered personages a more formal, less naturalistic rendering. Throughout the Fourth and Fifth Centuries these two styles—the continuation of classic naturalism and the new formalism

AN IVORY CASKET, *used as a jewel box, reflects a 10th Century revival of classical taste and themes in nonreligious objects. The rosette-framed panels contain scenes from Greek mythology.*

—existed side by side, mixing occasionally, but not too successfully.

In the Sixth Century, the age of Justinian, the first successful fusion of the styles took place. The style that resulted is most clearly seen in Early Byzantine ivory carvings and silverwork produced up until the early Eighth Century. These works took over from classical art its naturalistic figures and its general rhythmic balance of composition. The solidity and three-dimensionality of the classical figure, however, generally was subordinated to surface patterns in the treatment of drapery and hair, which were often rendered in linear, stylized fashion. For the modeled, three-dimensional human face of classical art, a more abstract face was substituted, flat and with the features indicated in only a summary way.

Even though this fusion of the classical and the abstract styles is found in most Early Byzantine ivories and silverwork, there are a number of works in these media—including the Barberini ivory plaque depicting a triumphant emperor *(page 152)*, and silver plates illustrating scenes from the life of David *(page 158)*—which clearly show that a refined classicism was still very much alive. These pieces, because of their exceptional purity of style, are among the greatest treasures of Early Byzantine art still in existence.

What is true for the Barberini ivory and the David plates, in fact, seems to hold true for most existing great works of Early Byzantine art; the finest pieces embody either a continuation of pure classicism or reliance on a pure abstract style. The high quality of the classical strain, on the one hand, is strikingly visible in the early Sixth Century mosaics in Sant' Apollinare Nuovo at Ravenna, with their lifelike and fully rounded figures, and in a small but remarkably detailed Seventh Century wooden panel of St. Peter, which is the precious possession of the monastery of St. Catherine at Mount Sinai in Egypt. Among the best examples of the abstract style, on the other hand, are the early Eighth Century frescoes of Santa Maria Antiqua at Rome. Their powerful, static figures are compactly arranged within the composition; they face directly forward, and are sharply delineated in dark lines with most subtleties of features omitted.

The great works of Early Byzantine art that remain are mainly those preserved far from Constantinople—at Ravenna, Mount Sinai, Rome and elsewhere in Europe. Undoubtedly they reflect the style and quality of similar works that must have once existed in the capital. Unfortunately, almost all Early Byzantine art in Constantinople was destroyed during the iconoclastic controversy that swept the empire between 726 and 843.

This great religious dispute, as we have seen, centered on the icon (Greek for "image"), which in Byzantine art is any representation, small or large, of a holy person that attempts to convey the individual's sanctity or worthiness. Icons were made in many media; they appear as often in Byzantine church frescoes and mosaics as they do in the form of small panel paintings.

Early in Byzantine history icons became firmly entrenched in everyday worship. But in the late Seventh Century a militant opposition developed to the practice of icon-worship, which many regarded as a dangerous form of idolatry.

When the iconoclasts gained ascendancy in 726, they enforced their opposition to icons by removing them from churches and destroying religious books in which they appeared. Furthermore, they insisted that only Christian symbolic art (a simple representation of the Cross, for example) or purely decorative art, such as patterns of foliage, be used for the walls of churches and the pages of manuscripts. In 843, however, the champions of icons brought iconoclasm to an end.

Justified and sanctioned, the icon came to play an even more prominent role in Byzantine art than it did before the iconoclastic controversy, particularly during the Middle Byzantine period of the late Ninth to early 13th Centuries. First of all, the icon gave Byzantine art its distinctive style, one that has become known as "hieratic," from the Greek word for "sacred." The icon demanded concentration on the essential to the exclusion of the less important and the extraneous. It was the sanctity or worthiness of a holy figure that was important; his human qualities were de-emphasized. Thus iconic portraits ignored the actual physical characteristics of the human form such as its mass and solidity, and played down human emotions in the faces. For this reason the bodies of figures in Middle Byzantine art seem two-dimensional, almost weightless, and they possess calm, almost bland, countenances.

Second, the manner in which a subject was represented was rigidly prescribed by tradition and did not change very much over the years. Each one of the saints had to be recognizable by distinctive features, such as his hair, cloak or beard; the Nativity was almost invariably shown as taking place in a cave; the compositions of more complex scenes were repeated almost line for line whether they were rendered in the Eighth Century or the 12th.

In addition, Byzantine artists employed certain compositional devices to concentrate the attention of the viewer. Perspective was largely ignored. The figures most directly involved in the subject of the scene—for example, Christ and John the Baptist in the depiction of the Baptism—were made larger than the auxiliary figures, such as angels, regardless of position. Furthermore, the scene was usually purged of any deep or naturalistic landscape, a neutral gold background taking its place. The total effect was calculated: it drew immediate attention to the picture's surface, and to the center of that surface, where the most important event was taking place.

In addition to the iconographic traditions of individual portraits and Biblical scenes, there evolved still another distinctive feature of Byzantine art: a system or order of decoration for an entire church interior. Individual mosaics or frescoes were placed around the walls of the church in such a way as to show clearly the relative importance of the figures and scenes in the hierarchy of Church doctrine. Thus, the Son of God was placed in the dome of the church, the highest and most celestial point. Below Him, in order of importance, ranked the angels, scenes of the major events in the Life of Christ, the Apostles, prophets and, finally, in the lowest places, the saints. Although no complete scheme or cycle of this hierarchical order remains in Constantinople itself, a magnificent example is preserved in the Church of Hosios Loukas in Greece (page 101).

All the main developments of this iconographic

art emerged and attained full strength during the century following the iconoclastic controversy, but not simultaneously. Standardized representations of holy figures and scenes, along with the hierarchical order of church decoration, appeared first in the late Ninth Century. The typical abstract or hieratic qualities of Middle Byzantine style did not make their appearance until the mid-10th Century.

The earliest works of Middle Byzantine church art seem to have been modeled on works of Justinian's reign, particularly on those Sixth Century works showing the classical strain—for example, the mosaics in Ravenna's Sant' Apollinare Nuovo. In the early 10th Century, during the rule of Constantine VII Porphyrogenitus, the classical strain was further purified to the extent that the art produced in his time represents a renaissance of antique style. This highly classical art continued on into the late years of the 10th Century, but mainly in such secular works as ivory jewel caskets. An exquisite example is the Veroli casket, now in the Victoria and Albert Museum, in which the subjects—scenes from mythology—as well as the style stem from classical antiquity.

From the late 10th Century on, however, the greater part of church art was in the sophisticated abstract style. Thus most of the religious ivories, manuscripts and works in precious metals of the late 10th to 12th Centuries display the elongated figures, bland features and intricate linearism of the hieratic convention.

With the conquest of Constantinople by the Crusaders in 1204, Byzantine art suffered a brief hiatus. The production of most art works seems to have ceased abruptly. Illuminated manuscripts, however, continued to be made, and their style shows no interruption in the Middle Byzantine style of the previous three centuries. In 1261 a Byzantine emperor once more resumed the throne, and from then until the mid-15th Century—the Late Byzan-

tine period—works of art were fewer and less varied than in earlier ages; in many cases they lacked the perfection and originality of Middle Byzantine creations. But the highest artistic standards were maintained in mosaics and in fresco paintings which—largely for reasons of economy—virtually replaced mosaics in church decoration as the Late Byzantine period progressed.

Unlike the Church art of earlier periods, that of Late Byzantine times became infused with a liveliness of style, and its subject matter broadened: artists no longer felt constrained to dwell so completely on the essentials of a subject; secondary figures crept into the scenes of the Life of Christ; the Death of the Virgin began to include the transportation of her soul to Heaven amid a host of attending angels. Figures in the scenes were no longer static. Christ, for example, was now depicted in action, literally pulling Adam out of Hell.

The closing era of Byzantine art saw a return to naturalism, but a naturalism of a new kind. Emphasis was now placed on emotions rather than on mere physical forms—on Christ's Passion, for example, and on the sorrow and tenderness of Mary. Both the purely naturalistic figures of classical art and the abstract, expressionless faces of the hieratic style were replaced by more humane and compelling features.

Throughout its thousand-year history Byzantine art influenced the art of Eastern and Western Europe, largely through the importation of Byzantine artists and works of art. Never was this influence more significant than in the 12th and 13th Centuries, a period that witnessed the widest diffusion of Byzantine art. To this era belong such mosaics as those in the Cathedrals in Torcello near Venice and at Monreale and Cefalù in Sicily. The glorious beginnings of the Renaissance—the age of Cavallini, Duccio and Giotto—rested largely on this finest flowering of Byzantine art.

A CHRIST IN MOSAIC *is restored by careful hands, which remove plaster that has hidden it for centuries.*

TRADITIONS OF BEAUTY

Over the long centuries of Byzantium's life, the hands of creative artists pressed into place the tiny bits of glass and stone that form mosaics. The hands of others carved exquisite ivories, painted frescoes, illuminated manuscripts, worked precious metals and wove silks. The mood of their art was reverent; their intent was to stimulate profound religious thought. The traditions they handed down flourished wherever the empire held sway: in Constantinople, Greece, the Balkans, Italy, Syria, Egypt. Today, in the finest of their surviving works—some of them only recently rediscovered behind the dirt and plastered-over walls of venerable churches—the techniques and achievements of these artists still evoke admiration.

AT NORMAL VIEWING DISTANCE, *Shadrach, Meshach and Abed-nego, the three holy children of the Bible, are seen in their fiery furnace. This mosaic, with its glittering gold background, is in the Church of Hosios Loukas in Greece. Outlines for mosaics were first made on the rough wet plaster, then the pieces were pressed into a layer of fine plaster to hold them in place.*

IN A CLOSE-UP VIEW *of one figure, the individual colors used to create overall effects become separately distinguishable. The face, outlined in dark stones, is fleshed out with bits of white and pink marble and modeled with greenish-gray pieces to suggest shadows. Reds and browns are used for the cloak and stylized hair. The golden pieces of the halo were made by annealing gold leaf to the bottom of clear glass. Other colors were baked into the glass when it was made.*

SEEN CLOSER STILL, *the face becomes an int cate pattern of tiny rectangles placed in orde ly lines. To make the pieces, called tessere slabs of stone and colored glass were brok up into cubes three eighths of an inch on side; odd sizes were used to fill awkward spo*

GREAT MOSAICS FROM TINY STONES

Mosaics, adorning the floors and walls of private villas and imperial palaces, attaining monumental magnificence on the vaults and domes of churches, were Byzantium's transcendent work. Most of these mosaics were made by sophisticated men—not, as a quick glance at some works might suggest, by primitives baffled by problems in perspective. Individuals and scenes were designed to be clear, simple and recognizable so they would have maximum impact when seen from a distance, as on the walls and higher vaultings of a church. Yet as the curious human eye comes closer and closer to the large and impassive mosaic eye, all manner of subtle touches are revealed: a gentle modeling achieved by curving the lines of the stone; a gradation of color attained by using stones of different hues; a glittering background enhanced by setting the cubes at different angles to the light.

EARLY BYZANTINE: *A Sixth Century Christ is rendered as a living, three-dimensional man.*   MIDDLE BYZANTINE: *An 11th Century Christ is reduced*

SUBTLE SHIFTS IN STYLE

Most Byzantine mosaics, particularly those of the middle centuries, were executed in a manner known as hieratic, meaning holy or sacred—a formalized, almost rigid, style designed not so much to picture men and events as to inspire reverence and meditation. One tradition ordained that "a man measure nine heads" (modern proportions make a man about seven

flat, almost abstract patterns.   LATE BYZANTINE: *A 13th Century Christ is natural again, but now shows a new depth and compassion.*

heads tall); that his hairline rise a nose's length above his forehead; and that "if the man is naked, four noses' lengths are needed for half his width." Pressure to preserve these and many other rules was as strong on the artist as the demand on the priest to guard unaltered the canon of the Mass, and for much the same reason: both men were keeping the sacred

mysteries. Nevertheless, many subtle changes in style took place during the long life of the hieratic school. The examples seen above demonstrate how Byzantine artists moved, during a thousand years of activity, from the classical influences of Greece and Rome through the asceticism of the East, and finally to a new and more deeply moving kind of naturalism.

149

FOURTH CENTURY CEMETERY GLASS FROM THE CATACOMBS

FIFTH CENTURY MOSAIC AT RAVENNA, ITALY

SEVENTH CENTURY WAX ON WOOD PANEL, MT. SINAI

10TH CENTURY IVORY MADE IN CONSTANTINOPLE

12TH CENTURY ENAMEL, NOW IN VENICE

13TH CENTURY FRESCO, YUGOSLAVIA

UNCHANGING PRECEPTS FOR PORTRAITURE

Artists were required by their clients—primarily the Church and the state—to make their pictures instantly recognizable to all beholders. One result of this policy was a portraiture that used a standardized human face to which was applied the distinguishing features for each Biblical personality. Thus, over the centuries St. Peter was always depicted wearing a rounded white beard, St. John the Baptist a scraggly one; St. Paul was always bald and St. Demetrios clad in a suit of mail. Color, too, was prescribed: Christ was to wear blue and gold before the Crucifixion and purple and gold after the Resurrection; the Blessed Virgin was to be clothed in blue and purple, St. Peter in gold and beige. Often these rules were ignored by the artist, but rules they remained, violable only by men who had first established their artistic worth in obeying them. When working for the Church, artists were also required to base their representations on approved authorities: an earlier image believed to be of heavenly origin, a description of the scene by a contemporary witness, or a passage from Holy Scripture.

THE FACE OF ST. PETER *was represented in many ways (left), from profiles in glass and mosaic to frescoes. But his distinguishing features remained virtually unchanged: curly hair, a forelock and a rounded white beard.*

ST. JOHN THE BAPTIST *is the same desert ascetic in three depictions. At the top he is shown in his role as baptizer; in the center as a saint to be venerated. In the bottom scene he is an intercessor at the Last Judgment.*

11TH CENTURY MOSAIC, DAPHNI, GREECE

12TH CENTURY MOSAIC, CONSTANTINOPLE

14TH CENTURY FRESCO, CONSTANTINOPLE

THE BARBERINI PLAQUE, *classical in style, is named for a family that once owned it.*

ARTISTRY IN IVORY

The Byzantines' love of luxury is evident in the many superb objects—altar furnishings, jewel boxes, plaques, triptychs—that they carved from elephant tusks and walrus teeth. Since the supply of ivory depended on trade with India, Africa and the Vikings, this was an expensive art, flourishing only in times of great prosperity. Many artistic influences played upon it. The Sixth Century plaque above, which celebrates an emperor's triumph, is descended in style from the imperial art of ancient Rome, while the equally exquisite 10th Century triptych at the right, religious in theme, is executed in the appropriate and more formal hieratic manner.

THE HARBAVILLE TRIPTYCH, *also named for former owners, shows in its center panel an enthroned Christ, flanked by Mary and St. John, above five of the Apostles. The side panels depict warrior saints and other holy figures.*

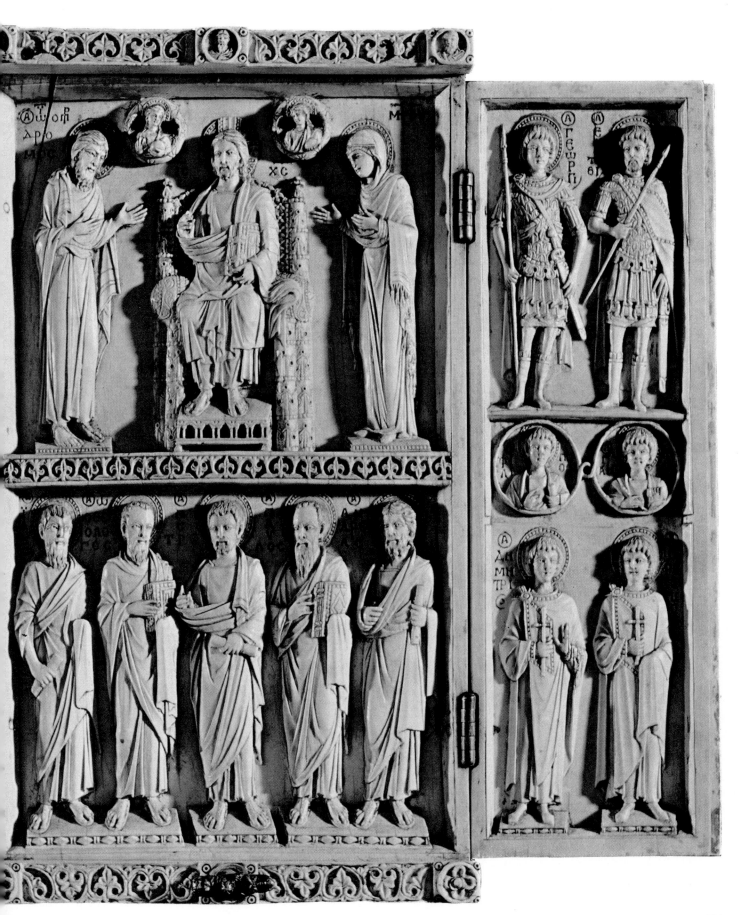

ILLUMINATIONS ROMANTIC AND SEVERE

The scribes who wrote Byzantium's precious manuscripts and the artists who illustrated them were practicing a highly developed art. The manuscripts were of two general types. In one, text pages, usually from the Bible, were interspersed with full-page illustrations that had only a casual relation to the text. The artists could follow their imaginations or borrow from the rich stores of pre-Christian art. In the painting at the left, from a famous Book of

Psalms now in Paris, this freedom is reflected in the use of an idyllic landscape and allegorical figures surrounding David as he composes his psalms. A stricter, Church-dictated approach is seen below in more literal miniatures from a synaxarion, a liturgical book used in the Mass, which offers a daily lesson from the life of that day's saint. Here, in keeping with the illumination's religious use, the spare, severe style demands the viewer's attention.

A COMPOSER AT WORK, *David strums his lyre in a fanciful pastoral scene (left) while Melodia, the personification of Music, looks over his shoulder and Echo peeks from behind a column. Seated below is a pagan mountain god.*

PROCLAIMING THE FAITH, *sacred figures are seen in two illuminated miniatures of hieratic style. In the top one, Christ reads from the Book of Isaiah before the synagogue at Nazareth. Below, St. Eumenius, Bishop of Gortyna, harkens to the Lord, whose commanding hand enters the picture from the upper left.*

MASTERWORKS
IN FRESCO

The glorious frescoes of the Church of St. Clement, in the Yugoslavian town of Ohrid, have only recently been restored to their original brilliance through the removal of six centuries of dirt. The figures in the apse and half dome of the sanctuary are dominated by the Virgin, who stands above a double Communion scene showing Christ giving bread on the left and wine on the right. Below are portraits of fathers of the Orthodox Church in bishops' robes; on the sides of the arch are heads of Old Testament figures.

Fresco painting, in which pigments are applied directly to the wet wall plaster, was practiced in Byzantium mainly after the 10th Century, often as a less expensive substitute for mosaics. But frescoes such as those in St. Clement are far more than bargain-rate art. For one thing, the artists were no longer anonymous servants of the Church, but men who signed their names to their works (Eutychius and Michael in this case). Moreover, although these artists retained some hieratic devices, they also made good use of the spontaneity that fresco painting allowed and established many local styles. Their best work, such as the frescoes shown here, compares in quality with the wall paintings of Pompeii and some of the mural masterworks of the Renaissance.

A SOLID SILVER PLATE, *made in Constantinople in the early Seventh Century, shows David meeting Saul. It was buried when Arab soldiers invaded Cyprus in 648 and was not unearthed again until 1902.*

SMALLER TREASURES

Along with its brilliance in major works, Byzantium gleamed with highly polished minor arts: golden cups and silver spoons, gem-encrusted jewelry, embroidered tapestries and fine enamels. Some objects were reserved for imperial use. But there was much for sale to the public and at night the taper-lit windows of the imperial workshops in Constantinople glittered with precious things to entice buyers. The violence of Byzantine history—including two thorough pillages of Constantinople itself—spared little of this art. Where it has survived, it is often thanks to the Crusader who carried these treasures off as spoils of war, or to the terrified Byzantine who buried them to prevent their theft.

A SILKEN TAPESTRY *depicts Mary listening to the angel who tells her that she will be the Mother of God. Silk making began in Justinian's time, with silkworm eggs smuggled from China by ingenious monks.*

A JEWELED RELIQUARY *(right) shows Christ at its center, surrounded by Mary, John the Baptist and the Apostles. Taken as war booty from the imperial treasury in 1204, it is now in a German cathedral.*

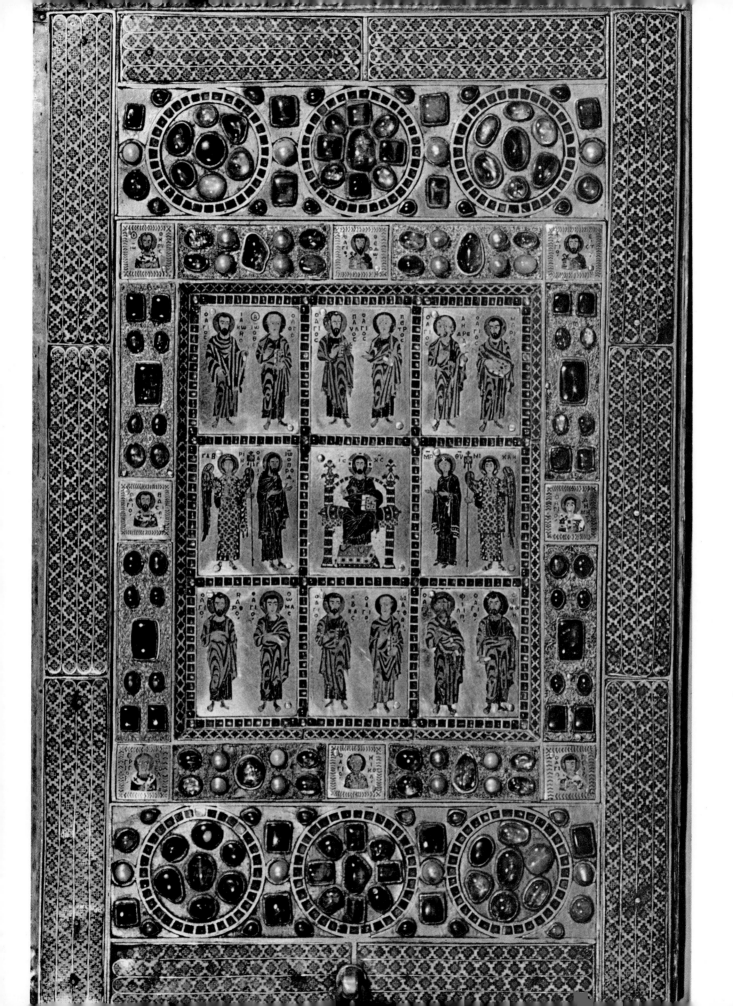

8
THE FINAL CENTURIES

That intelligent Byzantine philosopher and chronicler of the 11th Century, Michael Psellus, saw no signs of decline in the nation during his lifetime, though he found much to disparage. He deplored the excessive expenditures of the later members of the Macedonian imperial house, who vied with one another in building increasingly extravagant memorials to their reign. "The imperial treasury was opened up and the gold kept there was allowed to pour forth like a river," he wrote, and added that uncontrolled spending could be disastrous for the fortunes of the state. He also described a dangerous conflict for power between the civil aristocracy of the capital and the great landed nobility. Although he did not suggest that forces of disintegration were at work, Byzantium was already moving toward its downfall. Psellus perceived some of the causes, but without realizing that they might become fatal.

The chief factors that brought Byzantium to its doom after more than 1,000 years were the continuing struggles for power within the empire, and gradual alterations in the social structure that had bound all classes of society to the country. There were also external forces that helped bring about the downfall. One of these was the West's competition in trade, which led eventually to a severe drop in Byzantine commerce. Another was the increasingly frequent clashes between the Western Church at Rome and the Eastern Church at Constantinople, which in the long run worked to the empire's disadvantage. And finally, there were the Moslem Turks. It was Turkish power that in the end erased Constantinople as both an independent and a Christian power; even before that, the presence of the Turks exacerbated the ever-mounting crises of Byzantium.

In the middle of the 11th Century, none of this was evident. Inside Byzantium, in the years following the end of the Macedonian dynasty in 1056, the civil nobility of the capital and the large landowners, allied with the leadership of the army, contended for power. At first the civil nobility dominated. But in 1081 Alexius Comnenus succeeded in attaining the throne, and his success marked the triumph of the landowners and the army.

The reigns of Alexius Comnenus (1081-1118),

his son John II (1118-1143), and his grandson Manuel I (1143-1180) spanned a century. Manuel was a gifted man—soldier, statesman, theologian. He dreamed of restoring the lost might of Byzantium just as Justinian had dreamed of restoring that of the Roman Empire, and like Justinian he launched attacks on Italy itself, though without sustained success. Strongly attracted to the customs of the West, he introduced chivalric practices to the Byzantine court and appointed Latins to many positions of influence in the state. Though this revived contact with the West produced a stimulating ferment of ideas among the Byzantines, Manuel's reckless extravagance and the expense of his military enterprises brought the state to the verge of bankruptcy. As the tax burden on the peasantry mounted, many small landholders were forced to sell their farms to the increasingly powerful semifeudal magnates. It was during the reign of the Comnenus family, which itself had come from the ranks of the landed nobility, that the power of the landowning aristocracy grew to the point where, with increasing independence, it could oppose the central authority of the state.

At the same time, pressure from forces outside the empire increased. From the 10th Century onward the West had been stirred by the sight of Byzantine brocades, onyx cups, miniatures, reliquaries studded with jewels, and magnificent works in gold or enamel; such objects had been circulated by Italian and Jewish merchants through the castles and cloisters of France and England, the burgs of the Rhine and the palaces of Italy. To this traffic had been added Byzantium's own political and cultural propaganda, in the form of lavish and magnificent gifts to foreigners, all providing evidence of unlimited wealth and splendor.

Many a Western ruler was tempted by the lure of Constantinople. In the 11th Century, the most dangerous of these rulers to the Byzantines was Robert Guiscard, the energetic leader of the Normans. By 1071, Norman adventurers had occupied all the Byzantine possessions in southern Italy. Guiscard now planned to conquer the rest of the empire and seize the imperial crown for himself. To counter the Norman aggression, Alexius Comnenus, conscious of the weakness of his own land and naval forces, sought help from the Venetians.

Owing to the assistance of Venice and the fortuitous death of Guiscard at the height of the Norman attack, the Norman advance was checked. But the price the Venetians demanded for their aid was the concession of extensive trading privileges throughout the empire. This naturally provoked jealousy among the other Italian maritime republics. More important, it meant that a Western power had obtained a vital trading foothold within the empire itself. As Alexius' successors came to depend more and more on the use of Italian ships for Byzantium's defense, trading concessions had to be granted to the Genoese and the Pisans as well. Constantinople's grip on trade was weakened, and the rich tolls on which the imperial exchequer had so heavily relied soon dwindled into insignificance.

The commercial inroads of the Italians were accompanied by a steady worsening of the relations between the two Christian Churches. Some of the points of disagreement in this long dispute were purely theological (e.g., whether the Holy Spirit proceeded only from the Father, as the Orthodox Christians maintained, or from both the Father and the Son, as it was stated in the amended Latin creed). Other disputes were political, or quasi-political. The crowning of Charlemagne as emperor by the Pope in the year 800 had been taken at Constantinople as a deliberate attack on the universal status and authority of the Byzantine emperor. In the 11th Century the papacy began to press its claims to universal spiritual authority, asserting that the Byzantine Church too should be subject to the Roman See's divinely chosen primacy.

Rome and Constantinople also competed for jurisdictional rights over various peoples newly converted to Christianity. In the Ninth Century they argued over, and ultimately hindered the missions of, St. Cyril and St. Methodius in Moravia in Central Europe. A similar dispute concerning Bulgaria, also in the Ninth Century, was resolved in favor of Constantinople only when the Byzantines agreed to allow the Bulgarians to establish a semiautonomous Bulgarian archbishopric. And it was the question of jurisdictional rights over dioceses in Byzantine territories in southern Italy that was one of the immediate causes of the schism between the Churches of Rome and Constantinople in 1054.

The deterioration of relations between the two halves of Christendom eventually had a direct influence on the final fall of Byzantium to the Turks. As early as the Sixth Century the Byzantines had been in contact with the empire the Turks had established in Central Asia. In later centuries, as Turkish tribes were forced to move westward, these contacts increased. Two Byzantine emperors had in fact married princesses of one of the Turkish tribes—the cultivated Khazars, who had converted to Judaism after their migration to the area north of the Black Sea. Other Turkish tribes had supplied contingents of mercenaries to both the Byzantine emperor and the Arab caliph, who ruled his theocratic empire from Baghdad. Many of these mercenaries stayed on to settle within the borders of the Byzantine and the Arab empires, becoming Christians or Moslems accordingly.

It was the Turks living in the lands of the caliph who first became a threat to Byzantium, for as the central power of Baghdad in this area declined, the power of the Turks increased. The first Moslem Turk to build up a powerful state was a half-legendary prince by the name of Mahmud of Ghazni. By the beginning of the 11th Century Mahmud was in control of an empire that stretched from northeastern Persia to the Punjab. On his death, overlordship among the Turks who had settled in the realm of the caliph passed into the Seljuk family. The Turks continued their conquests and by the middle of the 11th Century the Seljuk ruler Tugrul had conquered not only the whole of Persia from the caliph but also the territory of Khorezm, lying east of the Caspian Sea. In 1055 the Seljuks marched on Baghdad, the seat of the caliphate. The city surrendered without a struggle, and the caliph bestowed the title of sultan and temporal control over his domains to the Seljuk chieftain, while he himself retained religious control.

Meanwhile, other Turkish warriors had been raiding Byzantine territories. The Byzantines were alarmed, and Emperor Romanus IV Diogenes decided to advance against them. The Byzantine and Turkish armies, led by Tugrul's successor, Alp Arslan, met at Manzikert in August 1071. In a battle of far-reaching consequences for Europe and for the world, the Byzantines were defeated and the Emperor was taken prisoner.

Alp Arslan was lenient and did not press his advantage. He released the Emperor on fairly easy terms and turned back to complete his conquest of Syria. But the southern and eastern borders of the Byzantine empire were now virtually defenseless, and the appetites of the Turkish border barons had been sharpened. These barons—they bore the title of *ghazi*, or warrior for the faith, and observed a semimystical discipline developed in the 10th and 11th Centuries—were professional raiders and fighters. Encountering little or no opposition, they penetrated into Byzantine territory, and settled the areas into which they advanced. Often the Christians fled before them, leaving their lands and villages unoccupied.

By the end of the 11th Century, the *ghazi* raiders had overrun the greater part of Anatolia, and

COLLAPSE OF THE EMPIRE

- Territories lost by 1092
- Territories lost by 1350
- Territories lost by 1402
- Territories lost by 1453
- ✗ Some important battlefields

only a few coastal districts remained in Byzantine hands. The Seljuk Turks themselves were alarmed at the *ghazis'* growing independence and power and sought to organize them into a single Islamic kingdom. When this had been done, in the early years of the 12th Century, the boundary between Byzantine and Turkish lands was fixed along a rough line which left the empire with the coastal districts and the fertile valleys of western Anatolia, and the Turks in control of the whole hinterland, with their capital at Konya.

One of the most fateful repercussions of the Byzantine defeat at Manzikert was that it aroused the West to the precarious position of Byzantium. As the victorious Seljuks went on to capture the Holy Land from the Arabs, Western alarm heightened. The idea of a crusade to liberate the holy places of Palestine began to grow—and the Roman papacy, anxious to expand its power, looked also to Byzantium as a land to be "saved."

In the decades following 1054 the Turkish triumphs in Asia Minor were interpreted by Rome as a form of divine retribution upon the Byzantines for the schism that became formal that year. "Great pain and universal sorrow obsess me," wrote

Pope Gregory VII to Hugh, Abbot of Cluny. "The Church of the Orient is moving further from the Catholic faith, and the devil, having killed it spiritually, causes its members to perish in the flesh by the sword of his henchmen lest at any time divine grace bring them to a better mind." In this spirit the Roman Church could view the return of any of Byzantium's imperial territories to papal jurisdiction as a victory over the powers of encroaching darkness, while Constantinople itself was seen as the vital key to papal dominion over Eastern Europe, Russia and the Near East. The West's secular rulers were no less tempted than the Pope by the prize of Byzantium.

In 1095 at the Council of Clermont, Pope Urban II exhorted the West to action. A year later a disorganized rabble of Crusaders led by Peter the Hermit managed to reach Anatolia, where they were easily killed off by the Turks. A few months later came real armies led by nobles of Norman and other stock. A few of the leaders were motivated by religious zeal, but more were driven by a spirit of adventure and a lust for gain. The Byzantines exacted a promise from the Crusaders that any former Byzantine cities recaptured from the

Turks should be returned to Constantinople's rule. The condition was honored for Nicaea and certain other places. But the Norman army retained Antioch after it was captured. Bohemund, son of that old anti-Byzantinist, Robert Guiscard, made himself master of Antioch and refused to hand it over. The Crusaders set up other principalities at Edessa, Jerusalem and Tripoli. But in 1137 the Emperor, John II, asserted his rights as ruler of Antioch, and in 1144 the Moslems recaptured Edessa.

In 1147, the Second Crusade was called forth by St. Bernard of Clairvaux and led by Conrad III of Germany and King Louis VII of France. It won no victories over the Moslems, but the political designs of the West against Byzantium began to show through more clearly. In the midst of the Crusade, the Norman contingent suddenly seized the Byzantine island of Corfu and, landing on the Greek mainland, captured Thebes and Corinth. King Louis of France at one moment seriously considered seizing Constantinople itself.

In 1187 the Moslems recaptured Jerusalem, the Holy City, and two years later the Third Crusade set forth. It failed to regain Jerusalem—but again a threat was made against Constantinople, this time by the German king. During a dispute with the Byzantine Emperor, Frederick Barbarossa actually ordered that preparations be made for an attack on the city, but the Emperor yielded to Frederick's demands and the threat was averted.

At last in 1203, the Fourth Crusade, originally dispatched for Egypt and the Holy Land, was actually diverted to Constantinople. The diversion was engineered by the Venetians. The elderly doge of Venice, Enrico Dandolo, hated the Byzantines: 30 years earlier, while being held as a hostage in Constantinople, he had been blinded by the Greeks through exposure to a concave mirror which strongly reflected the sun's rays. Apart from motives of revenge, Dandolo coveted the economic advantages

Venice would gain from Byzantium's conquest. The ostensible excuse for the diversion was the restoration of a deposed emperor to the Byzantine throne. The net result, after a succession of complicated events—battles, betrayals and all manner of chicanery—was that in 1204 the city was taken by the Crusaders and pillaged mercilessly.

The Emperor Alexius V Ducas Mourtzouphos fled lest, as Senator Nicetas Choniates tells us, he "fall into the teeth of the Latins as a tidbit or dessert." Behind him, his people suffered at the hands of their fellow Christians the classic fate of losers. Churches, palaces, monasteries and libraries, as well as the fine villas of the rich and the hovels of the poor, were indiscriminately sacked by soldiers and clerics alike. The good women of Byzantium were hard put to save their virtue. A prostitute was placed upon the throne in Hagia Sophia and set to singing drunken masses to which the victors danced. Altars were turned into dicing tables where frenzied soldiers gambled with their loot.

Three times during this furious rapine fire swept the city, destroying much of the accumulated art treasure of nine centuries. The voice of Nicetas rose in lament: "Oh, city, city, eye of all cities, subject of narratives over all the world, spectacle above the world, supporter of churches, leader of faith, guide of orthodoxy, protector of education, abode of all good! Thou hast drunk to the dregs the cup of the anger of the Lord and hast been visited with fire fiercer than that which in days of yore descended upon the five cities."

What was not destroyed by fire or vandalism was carted off. No one, wrote Villehardouin, a leader of the Crusaders, could possibly count the gold and silver, the plate and jewels, the samite and silks, the mantles of squirrel fur, ermine and miniver found by the Westerners; not since the world was created was so much contained in a single city. The treasure was taken off and has since filtered to all corners of Europe. Today one goes to the obscure town of Limburg on Lahn in Germany to inspect a Byzantine reliquary, to Venice to see Byzantine chalices and gold vessels and to other cities for other treasures.

As the empire collapsed, members of the former Byzantine court managed to establish themselves in three separate principalities, at Nicaea, in western Anatolia; on the southeast shores of the Black Sea and in Epirus, on the western coast of the Balkan peninsula. The remainder of the empire was partitioned among Venice and the Latin princes. The Venetians acquired concessions that insured them the entire Eastern trade, and they established colonies along the coast and on many of the islands. In the European territories of the empire a number of petty, semifeudal dependencies were set up in vassalage to Baldwin of Flanders, who with great pomp was crowned emperor of the Latin Empire of Constantinople. The Latin conquerers, however, proved unable to retain their gains. The local population grew increasingly restive as the hated Roman Church was forced upon them, and Baldwin and his successors had difficulty keeping their vassals in check.

Meanwhile, one of the three Byzantine kingdoms, Nicaea, was becoming more and more powerful. In July 1261, the Nicaean ruler, Michael Palaeologus, succeeded in capturing Constantinople. He was assisted by Genoa, Venice's rival for the Eastern trade. The Latin-installed emperor and patriarch fled, together with the Venetian trader-colonists.

The Byzantine empire now entered on the final phase of its history under the founder of its last —and, as events proved, its longest-lived—dynasty, the Palaeologus. A crippled and sadly reduced empire it was; the two final centuries, though they were brilliant intellectually and artistically, were little more than years of rear-guard actions against overwhelming odds. The empire Michael Palaeolo-

gus regained was confined to Constantinople, the northwest corner of Anatolia and a belt stretching across the center of the Balkans. Italians, particularly the Genoese, still dominated the empire's trade. Latin lords and Venetian traders managed to retain their holdings on the Greek mainland and the islands.

The authority of the central government was crippled, and the workings of the administrative machinery now largely depended on the cooperation of the virtually independent landowners and local governors. Continuing civil wars and dynastic quarrels further weakened the state (John V, though he reigned for 50 years, was deposed three times, by his father-in-law, son and grandson in turn). The Black Death, striking in 1347, carried off almost two thirds of Constantinople's population. By the end of the 14th Century the residents of the city numbered only about 100,000—one sixth its population two centuries earlier. As money grew short, the splendor of the Byzantine court vanished. "The jewels in the crowns were glass, the robes not real cloth-of-gold but tinsel, the dishes copper, while all that appeared to be rich brocade was only painted leather," wrote a contemporary observer.

Most ominous of all, a new Turkish power had been built up in northwestern Anatolia, ready to break into Europe. This was the Ottoman emirate. Although initially subjects of the Seljuk empire, the Ottoman Turks had won their independence as the Seljuk empire disintegrated under the impact of the Mongol invasions. In 1301 the Ottomans gained a first victory over the Byzantines at Baphaeum, between Nicaea and Nicomedia. In 1326 Brusa was captured, then Nicaea in 1329 and Nicomedia in 1337. In 1356 Ottoman troops crossed the Dardanelles and invaded Europe. By 1362 they were masters of western Thrace, and in 1365 they established their capital at Adrianople. In 1387

Salonika fell. The Turks defeated the Serbs at Kossovo in 1389, and in 1394 they ravaged the Peloponnese. By 1397 all that was left to the Byzantines was the city of Constantinople and a small area north of it, as well as some territory in the Peloponnese. The Turks then enveloped Constantinople and demanded its surrender. The city was saved by the advance of the Mongols under Tamerlane, who met and defeated the Ottoman forces at Ankara in July of 1402.

There was a breathing space now for Constantinople. Dynastic quarrels broke out among the Ottomans. They might have provided an opportunity for the Byzantines to recoup some of their losses. But they could not do so without Western assistance, and the condition for that was submission to Rome.

Over the years attempts had been made to bring about a reconciliation between the two Christian Churches. Michael VIII Palaeologus had committed his people to union with Rome at the Council of Lyons in 1274, only to have the union repudiated by his son, Andronicus II. In 1369, the Emperor, John V, had personally submitted to the Pope in Italy. But the majority of the clergy and people were too loyal to the Orthodox Church to think of making theological concessions for political ends, and memories of the Fourth Crusade had left them understandably suspicious of Latin motives. "Better the Sultan's turban than the Cardinal's hat"—a slogan attributed to Lucas Notaras, Byzantium's last Grand Admiral of the Fleet—expressed the popular attitude.

In 1413 the dynastic struggles among the Turks subsided with the accession of a new sultan, and in 1422 the Turks were again at the walls of Constantinople. A revolt in Anatolia saved the situation this time, but the Turkish army again ravaged the Peloponnese. The Emperor, John VIII Palaeologus, decided to make one more effort to enlist Western aid. Taking with him a number of bishops and theologians, he sailed to Italy and met with representatives of the Latin Church, first at Ferrara and then at Florence.

After endless debate a declaration of union between the Orthodox and Latin Churches was signed in 1439. Though some of the Orthodox representatives did not endorse the declaration, the Pope was encouraged. And the failure of a Turkish attempt to capture Belgrade in 1440 provoked him to preach another crusade against the Turks. It was to be led by King Vladislav of Poland and Hungary. Troops recruited by the Pope in the West were commanded by a papal legate, Cardinal Julian Cesarini. In 1444, the crusading force reached Varna, on the shores of the Black Sea, and was attacked by the Turks. The Crusaders were routed, and both King Vladislav and Cardinal Cesarini were killed. In 1448, another Hungarian force was defeated, this time on the plain of Kossovo. It was the final Western attempt to support the dying empire. The last years of Byzantium had come.

In 1451, a new Sultan, Mehmet II, inherited the Turkish throne and at once began preparation for the capture of Constantinople. To make sure that the strength and magnitude of the city's walls would not thwart the attack, Mehmet enlisted the skill of a Hungarian engineer, Urban, whose services had been turned down by the Byzantines because they could not afford to pay him. The engineer, offered every facility by the Turks, provided the Sultan's army with cannon of large caliber, which were to be big enough to smash the massive masonry of the walls. The largest of these cannon was a monster for its time: its barrel measured 26 feet in length and it fired balls weighing 1,200 pounds.

Mehmet diligently trained his Janissaries. These troops were made up of men born to the Sultan's Christian subjects. Every Christian family in Turkish dominions was forced to hand over any male child demanded by the Sultan's officials. The boys were brought up in special schools, and most of them were destined for the Sultan's guard regiments. They had their own barracks, were forbidden to marry, and constituted an élite, religious-military fraternity, with ideals of service and dedication similar to those of Western orders like the Templars.

Mehmet took two years to complete his preparations. On March 23, 1453, he set out from Adrianople. On the fifth of April he arrived outside the walls of Constantinople, where the bulk of his army had already taken up its positions.

The city was ruled by Constantine XI Palaeologus. He had been crowned at Mistra, in the Peloponnese, and shortly afterward had taken up residence at Constantinople. That city, weakened, impoverished, reduced, was virtually all that was left of his empire. There was scant prospect of foreign aid, though toward the end the Pope dispatched three galleys filled with arms and food, which arrived in time to be of use. After prolonged debate, Venice sent two transports, and later 15 galleys, but these ships did not leave Venice until after the siege was well under way, and they never did reach Constantinople.

Constantine rallied to the defense of the capital a force comprising all the city's able-bodied inhabitants. But of these 5,000 Byzantines and 2,000 foreigners, only a small proportion were professional military men. The foreigners were mostly Venetian and Genoese, the latter under the command of the brilliant Giovanni Giustiniani Longo. The defenders were well armed with javelins, arrows, muskets and mangonels for casting stones, but they faced a force at least 80,000 strong.

On April 6 the Sultan brought some of his cannon into action. Five days later, the great bombardment began. It continued with hardly a pause for the next six weeks. The defense was heroic. Not only did the defenders keep ceaseless watch all day, at night they succeeded in repairing the breaches in the walls. On April 18 a first assault by Turkish troops was repulsed. On April 22, however, the Sultan captured the Golden Horn by a prodigious combination of engineering and tactical surprise.

The Turkish fleet had previously tried to break through the floating boom stretched across the entrance to the Horn, but had been beaten back by the handful of Christian ships guarding it. The defeat had humiliated the Sultan. It was probably an Italian in his camp who suggested the possibility of hauling the ships overland from the Bosporus and insinuating them into the Horn behind its defenses. In Italy, the Venetians had recently dragged an entire fleet over the flat terrain that separated the River Po from Lake Garda. But never before had this been done on ground where all of the ridges were at least 200 feet above sea level. Nevertheless, Mehmet was determined, and he had ample men and material at his command. It took several weeks to lay more than a mile of roadway between the Bosporus and the Horn. Then, on April 21, the work assumed a frantic pace as thousands of laborers were drafted into the final preparations. To divert the attention of the Christians, the Sultan's cannon fired continuous volleys at the entrance to the Horn and the black smoke billowed up the Bosporus, helping to hide the activities there.

At dawn the following day a fantastic procession began. More than 70 of the Turkish ships in the Bosporus had been tied to wheeled cradles and dragged to shore. Teams of oxen were harnessed to the bows and squads of men helped push and pull along the sides. Slowly the vessels creaked up over the ridges, to the eerie accompaniment of fifes and drums. In each galley the sails were fully hoisted, ready for sea, and the oarsmen sat at their

places and pulled their oars through the air to a beat given by officers who paced alongside. The sight of this monstrous flotilla lumbering down the slopes and slithering into the Golden Horn numbed Constantinople's defenders. The city's long and vulnerable stretch of walls lining the Horn was no longer safe from attack. Having surrounded the capital by land and sea, the Turks in early May again attacked a section of the landward walls, only to be repulsed twice by the desperate valor of the Byzantines.

On May 25 the Sultan made a proposal for peace: he would spare the city on condition that an annual tribute be paid; alternatively, the citizens could have free passage to safety if they gave up the city. Both offers were rejected.

The Turks, discouraged because their seven-week siege had not yet succeeded, almost decided to withdraw. But after a pause the assault was renewed. Toward dusk on the 29th the Sultan addressed his ministers and his army leaders. He reminded them of the sacred prophecies that the Faithful should take the city; he spoke to them of its treasures, its palaces, its churches filled with silver and gold and precious stones, its fine gardens, its girls and young men. Those who died fighting for the Faith would enter directly into Paradise. Those who lived would have the traditional three days to pillage the city.

Inside Constantinople on that same day a solemn procession was held. Icons, the bones of saints and golden and jeweled crosses were borne round the city's walls. Soldiery and populace were blessed. Afterward, the Emperor addressed his commanders and chief citizens. He told them that the great trial was upon them, that, like himself, they must be ready to die, and that with God's help they still might triumph. It was now evening. All who could be spared from the defenses and who were still able to move repaired to the great church of Hagia Sophia. Patriarch and cardinal, Orthodox and Latin clergy, Emperor and nobles, soldiers and citizens, Greeks, Italians and Catalans—all took part in what was to be the last Christian service to be held in the church that for so long had stood as the symbol and heart of Byzantium's sacred Christian empire. When the service was over, each man returned to his post.

Giustiniani and his men, Italians and Greeks, took up their positions between the inner and outer walls opposite the weak spot from which the spearhead of the attack was expected. As they passed through the inner walls, the gates were locked behind them, making retreat impossible. Later that night the Emperor made his final tour of inspection. Then he too took up his station.

Shortly before 2 a.m. the assault began. To the clash of cymbals, the shrill notes of fifes, the cries of the soldiers and the thunder of cannon, wave after wave of Turks attacked, only to be beaten back. It seemed that the city might again be saved. But by mistake a small gate—a sally-port—had been left open in the outer walls. Some Turks found it and entered. Then Giustiniani was wounded, and although the Emperor begged him not to leave his post he was carried from the field and down to a Genoese ship. Many of his Genoese troops left with him. Outside the walls the Sultan noticed the confusion, and once more he ordered his Janissaries to charge. This time they were successful. They forced their way over the outer wall and reached the inner wall. A Turkish flag was flown from one of the towers, and the cry went up that the city was lost. Constantine XI Palaeologus, the last of the Byzantine emperors, knew that the end had come. Dismounting from his horse and casting his royal insignia from him, he flung himself into the thick of the advancing Janissaries, never to be seen again.

That afternoon the Sultan made his entry, escorted by his bodyguard of Janissaries. The three-day pillage permitted by Islamic tradition was already under way. When he reached the gates of Hagia Sophia the Sultan dismounted, stooped down at the threshold and scooped up a handful of earth, which he let fall on his turbaned head as an act of humiliation before the God who had brought him victory. Later he entered the deserted halls and galleries of the half-ruined imperial palace. As he gazed about him he murmured the words of a Persian poet: "The spider weaves the curtains in the palace of the Caesars; the owl calls the watches in Afrasiab's towers."

With the fall of the Byzantine capital, Byzantium had ceased to exist as a political entity. As heir to and preserver of the cultural tradition of the ancient Greco-Roman world, and as the bridge between that world and the modern world that grew out of the Renaissance, Byzantium had fulfilled its historical role. Its mission as an Orthodox Christian state, inspired by the vision of uniting all mankind into a single human society under the protection of the Cross, had to all intents and pur-

poses been terminated when Constantinople was sacked during the Fourth Crusade. But Byzantium had set the seal of its civilization on the whole Balkan world. In its own lands it survived in the threnes of the Greek ballad-makers, in the memory and ritual of the Orthodox Church, in the patient devotion of village priest or monk from the Holy Mountain of Athos. Some 400 years later, in 1821, the Greeks were to rise once more against their Turkish overlords and to lay the foundations of the modern Greek kingdom.

One Orthodox Christian state, however, still kept its independence. The conquering Sultan had scarcely given a thought to Russia, in many ways the principal heir to the historical mission of Byzantium. It was to Byzantium that Russia owed its conversion to Christianity. This faith Russia preserved. Though the sacred Orthodox empire and its Emperor had fallen, the mission of both went to Russia by inheritance.

Dynastically the claim could be supported by the fact that Ivan III of Moscow had married Princess Sophia of the Palaeologus house. But, as with Byzantium itself, what was more important than a dynastic link was the force of the idea, of the mystical vision of a sacred Christian society under the rule of a single semidivine emperor. This led to the assumption by the Russian ruler of the imperial Byzantine title of "Autocrat"; to the modeling of the Russian coronation ceremony on the Byzantine example; and to the adoption by the Russians of the double-headed eagle of the house of Palaeologus.

The historical implementation of the idea of the theocratic state—inherited from Rome and given a Christian form by Byzantium—lasted until July 16, 1918. On that night, the last Russian Czar, Nicholas II, and his family, were killed by the Bolsheviks at Ekaterinburg—and after 1,600 years the Byzantine political heritage had come to an end.

THE DOUBLE-HEADED EAGLE, *emblem of Byzantium, flies over a monastery on the Greek island of Patmos.*

STRONGHOLDS OF BYZANTIUM

The Byzantine tradition lives on today in Orthodox monasteries scattered far and wide throughout the eastern Mediterranean. Originally these monasteries were built like fortresses and situated in inaccessible places—on islands, on mountaintops and in the desert—in order to protect them from the attacks of Arab pirates, Crusaders and marauding Turks. In recent centuries, however, this isolation has served to protect the religious communities from the inroads of the modern world. Immune to change, Orthodox monks still paint icons, display the imperial flag *(above)*, remember Byzantine emperors in their prayers, and tell time, in true Roman fashion, not by clocks but by the elevation of the sun.

A RELIGIOUS OASIS

One of the world's first monasteries, St. Catherine's, lies at the foot of Mount Sinai on Egypt's Sinai Peninsula, where it has functioned for 1,400 years as a remote outpost of Byzantine Orthodoxy. Built by the Emperor Justinian in the Sixth

Century, St. Catherine's was designed to house pilgrims who came from every corner of Christendom to worship at the place where Moses, according to the Old Testament, received the Ten Commandments from God. St. Catherine's original walls still stand. Descendants of the Bedouin servants whom Justinian first attached to St. Catherine's still work for the monks, and modern scholars study illuminated manuscripts that were presented centuries ago as gifts from the throne.

HOLY MOUNTAINS

After its Third Century beginnings in Egypt, monasticism spread over all of Byzantium: by the Eighth Century tens of thousands of men lived as monks. A monastery usually began when a hermit, living in a cave or a mountain hut, attracted a band of pious followers, who eventually organized into formal communities such as those at Meteora in the plains of central Greece *(above)* or at Mount Athos *(right)*. Isolated on a narrow peninsula in the Aegean, the 20 monasteries and 200 hermitages of Mount Athos continue to function under the provisions of ancient imperial charters and the jurisdiction of the Patriarch of Constantinople.

AN AERIAL RETREAT, *the monastery of Roussanou (left), crowns a hilltop at Meteora on the Greek mainland. Once such places could be reached only when monks lowered ladders or nets; now steps lead to the peaks.*

CLIFF DWELLINGS *(right), the caves and huts of hermits, dot the southern tip of Athos peninsula in Greece. Hermits, who were the first religious inhabitants of Athos, started coming to the peninsula in the Ninth Century.*

THE GREAT LAVRA, *oldest monastery on Mount Athos, was founded in 963 A.D. on the site of a temple to the Greek goddess Athena. The Great Lavra defended itself with cannon more than once against attackers. Today its rambling galleries and cells house 80 monks.*

A HERITAGE OF WORK AND PRAYER

"Think much and talk little," instructed Saint Basil, the father of Byzantine monasticism, and the Orthodox monk still pursues this contemplative ideal of 16 centuries ago. Most monks espouse a simple, unquestioning faith and all are pledged to uphold the three vows of poverty, chastity and obedience. Poverty is profound, for even though a few brothers may keep the profits from the sale of their handicrafts, almost all dwell in stark cells and eat frugal meals. To ensure chastity, most monasteries forbid women within their walls. Obedience is cultivated by a rigorous daily schedule of fasting, meditating and praying. In fact, prayers are said all through the night; many men never stop praying except to sleep—and then for no more than two hours at a time.

KEEP IN WORK *(left), a brother of Mount Athos carves a wooden vase inscribed with the Greek word for "holy." Almost every monk has an assigned job; some are blacksmiths, tailors or artists, while others farm, fashion religious objects or repair buildings.*

A SILENT MOMENT *during the day's activities occurs as a monk reads his breviary at St. John's Monastery on Patmos Island. The Emperor Alexius donated the island for the monastery in 1088. When Constantinople fell 400 years later, hundreds of refugees fled to Patmos and settled close to St. John's walls.*

LIVING WITH THE PAST

Life on Mount Athos, the capital of Byzantine monasticism, is a total and intentional anachronism. None of the monasteries was built after the 16th Century; the monks' "angelical habits" date from the imperial age. When the members

of the Dionysiou monastery eat *(above)*, they sit beneath Byzantine murals of saints and martyrs and listen to a brother read a traditional lesson against gluttony. The wine they drink traces back to an even more remote, mythical time: Dionysus himself, the Greek god of wine, supposedly planted the monastery's vineyard. So avidly do the monks hold to their past that even now in formal letters they call their establishments "the Imperial Monasteries of the Holy Mountain."

A CONTINUING CALL TO PIETY

During the last 50 years the fortunes of Mount Athos have entered upon a steep decline. Only 1,500 monks inhabit the community's several monasteries now, one-fifth of the number who lived thus at the turn of the century. Before World War I 3,500 monks came from Russia alone, but today the Russian monastery numbers only about 30 survivors. Moreover, every year fewer recruits come from Greece, Romania and Bulgaria. But this "Ark of Byzantium," as the monks call Mount Athos, has experienced lean times before and gone on to prosper. As the world wearies of its own complexities, Orthodox monks hope the disillusioned will return to the simple virtues of their holy faith.

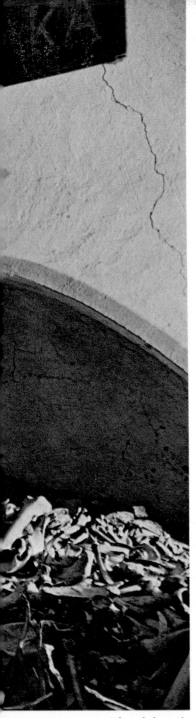

A CHARNEL HOUSE at *Athos shelters the bones of former monks. Because burial space is scarce, bones are exhumed after three years and piled here. Biographies of some brothers are written on their skulls.*

ANNOUNCING PRAYERS, *a monk strikes a mallet against a long wooden gong, or semantron, as he crosses a monastery courtyard at Athos. Semantrons are holdovers from a time when bells did not exist.*

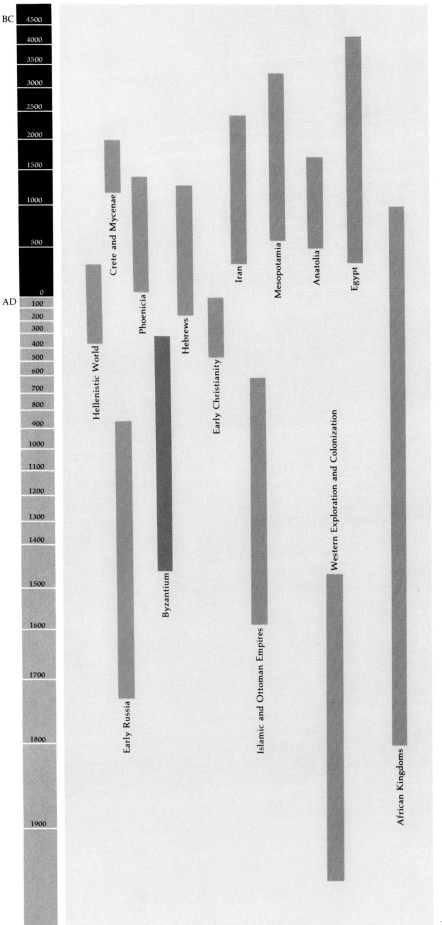

CROSSROAD CIVILIZATIONS BETWEEN EAST AND WEST

The chart at right is designed to show the duration of the Byzantine empire, and to relate it to others in the "Crossroad" group of cultures that are considered in one major group of volumes of this series. This chart is excerpted from a comprehensive world chronology which appears in the introductory booklet to the series. Comparison of the chart seen here with the world chronology will enable the reader to relate the crossroad civilizations to important cultures in other parts of the world.

On the following pages is a chronological listing of important events that took place in the period covered by this book.

CHRONOLOGY: *A listing of significant events during the Byzantine empire*

300

324   Constantine I becomes sole emperor of the Roman Empire

325   First Ecumenical Council is called at Nicaea

330   Constantinople, the new capital of the Roman Empire, is dedicated

337   Constantine the Great dies

361   The Harbor of Julian is constructed at Constantinople

363   Treaty with Persians results in loss of the empire's Armenian lands and much of those in the Mesopotamian region

374   St. Ambrose becomes Bishop of Milan

378   The Aqueduct of Valens is completed in the center of Constantinople

379   Theodosius I begins his 16-year rule, establishing the Theodosian Dynasty

390   The obelisk of Theodosius is erected in the Hippodrome

395   Arcadius becomes emperor

400

404   St. John Chrysostom is exiled because of his criticism of Empress Eudoxia; in the resulting riots, Hagia Sophia is burned

408   Theodosius II succeeds Arcadius

410   Rome is sacked by Alaric the Visigoth

413   Construction of Constantinople's triple walls is begun under Theodosius II

447   The walls of Constantinople are damaged by earthquake

455   Rome is sacked by the Vandals

463   The monastery of St. John of Stoudion is founded

474   Zeno marries Ariadne, daughter of Leo the Wise, and begins his rule

476   The last Western Emperor, Romulus Augustulus, is deposed by Odovar the Ostrogoth, and the imperial office in the West comes to an end

491   Anastasius I marries the Empress Ariadne, becomes emperor and reigns for 27 years

500

518   Justin I, son of an Illyrian peasant, takes the Byzantine throne

525   Antioch is destroyed by earthquake

527   Justinian, nephew of Justin I, becomes emperor and reigns for 38 years with his wife, Theodora; Constantinople reaches its cultural and economic zenith

527   The Church of Saints Sergius and Bacchus is erected

529   The Code of Justinian is adopted as the basis of Byzantine law

532   Hagia Sophia and other buildings in Constantinople are severely damaged by fire during the Nika riots; construction is begun on present Hagia Sophia; underground cistern and St. Savior in Chora are built

565   Justin II ascends the throne as emperor

578   Tiberius I Constantine, adopted son of Justin II and the Empress Sophia, becomes emperor

590   Gregory the Great becomes pope in Rome

600

610   Heraclius begins his rule of 31 years, distinguishes himself as a military hero in wars against the Persians

614   Jerusalem is captured by the Persians

626   Constantinople is attacked by the Avars

635   Arab conquest of Persia is begun

638   Jerusalem falls to the Arabs under Caliph Omar I

641   Arabs begin their conquest of Egypt

649   The Arabs' first naval expedition goes to sea against Byzantium

668   Emperor Constans II is murdered in his bath at Syracuse by a member of his entourage

668   Constantine IV becomes emperor

673   Arabs begin their first attack on Constantinople

697   Carthage, the last Byzantine stronghold in Africa, falls to the Arabs

700

717   Arabs begin another siege of Constantinople, but are defeated by the emperor-general Leo III, who reigns thereafter for 24 years

c.726   The iconoclastic controversy begins

732   Charles Martel is victorious over the Arabs at Poitiers

750   The Umayyad Caliphate collapses and is succeeded by the Abbasid Caliphate

751   Ravenna is captured by the Lombards, and the Byzantine exarchate comes to an end

762   Baghdad is founded by the Caliph el Mansur

780   Constantine VI becomes emperor

787   Seventh and last Ecumenical Council recognized by the Eastern Church meets in Nicaea and condemns hostility to icons as heresy

797   The politically ambitious Irene, mother of Constantine VII, blinds her own son to become sole ruler, calling herself "emperor"

800

800   The imperial office in the West is revived by the coronation of Charlemagne

802   Palace revolution deposes Irene and proclaims Nicephorus emperor

813   Leo V the Armenian ascends the throne

815   The second phase of the iconoclast synod takes place in Constantinople

820   Phrygian Michael II succeeds the murdered Leo V on Christmas

829   Reign of Theophilus begins and coincides with period of Muslim culture's greatest influence on Byzantium

842   The iconoclastic controversy comes to an end; Constantinople enjoys a renaissance of the arts

860   The Russians make their first attack on the Byzantine capital and are repulsed

867   Basil I founds the Macedonian Dynasty

900

904 Arabs seize Thessalonica, the second greatest city of the empire

913 The emperor-scholar, Constantine VII Porphyrogenitus, begins his reign

927 Peace treaty achieved between Bulgars and Byzantium

941 Russians make surprise attack and lay waste to Asiatic shore of Bosporus

944 Threatening battle forces of Russia's Prince Igor leads to commercial treaty with the Russians

948 Romanus I, one of Byzantium's greatest rulers, dies in exile as a monk

957 Russian Princess Olga is feted at imperial court

963 Nicephorus II Phocas gains the throne through his marriage to the Empress Theophano, widow of Romanus II

969 John I Tzimisces becomes emperor by marrying Theodora, sister of Romanus II

976 The last great ruler in the Macedonian Dynasty, Basil II, ascends the throne

1000

1017 Basil conquers the Bulgarian kingdom and annexes its territories

1025 Basil dies and the heroic age of Byzantium is concluded

1028 St. Savior Pantepopte is built and mosaics are restored in Hagia Sophia

1054 The Byzantine Church breaks with Rome

1064 Hungarians occupy Belgrade

1067 Turks storm Caesarea

1071 Byzantium is overcome by the Seljuk Turks at the Battle of Manzikert; Bari is captured by the Normans and the last Byzantine stronghold in southern Italy is lost

1081 Alexius I Comnenus becomes emperor, establishing the Comneni Dynasty

1081 The imperial court moves to the newly enlarged Blachernae Palace

1096 The First Crusade is launched

1099 The Kingdom of Jerusalem is established by the Crusaders

1100

1111 Byzantines grant important trading rights to Pisans

c.1120 The monastery of St. Savior Pantocrator is founded

1147 The Second Crusade begins

1149 Byzantines, aided by Venetians, retake Corfu from Normans

c.1150 The walls of Manuel I are built to enclose the Blachernae Palace

1171 Venetians throughout the empire are arrested and their properties confiscated

1180 The Serbian monarchy is established by Stephen Nemanja

1185 Andronikos I is tortured to death

1186 The second Bulgarian empire is founded

1187 Jerusalem is captured by Saladin

1189 The Third Crusade is launched

1200

1201 The Fourth Crusade begins

1204 Constantinople is captured by troops of the Fourth Crusade; Alexius Comnenus founds the state of Trebizond, and Theodore Lascaris establishes the Greek empire of Nicaea

1204 Theodore I Lascaris becomes the first of the Greek emperors of Nicaea

1222 John III Dukas Vatazes marries Irene, daughter of Theodore I Lascaris, and rules for 32 years

1261 Michael VIII Palaeologus takes Constantinople from Latin control and establishes the dynasty of the Palaeologi

1274 Byzantine Emperor Michael VIII comes to terms with Pope Gregory X, acknowledging papal primacy and the Roman faith

c.1290 St. Savior in Chora is restored and mosaics installed; the Pareiclesion Chapel is added to the Church of the Blessed Virgin in Pammakaristos

1300

1300 Ottoman Turkish conquests begin, diminishing the Byzantine empire

1329 The Turks capture Nicaea and other cities to become masters of Asia Minor

1346 Genoese take the important trading center of Chios

1349 The Tower of Galata is built in Constantinople

1354 The Ottoman Turks take Gallipoli

1359 Ottoman Turks invade to the walls of Constantinople

1389 The Serbian empire falls to the Turks at the Battle of Kossovo

1391 Manuel II begins his 34-year reign

1393 Bulgarian Empire subjugated by the Ottomans who hold that country for the subsequent 500 years

1397 Constantinople is attacked by the Ottoman Sultan Bayazid

1400

1402 The Turks are defeated by Timur at the Battle of Ankara

1422 Constantinople is attacked by Ottoman Sultan Murad II

1425 John VIII becomes emperor and rules for 23 years

1430 Ottoman forces capture Salonika

1438 The Council of Ferrara attempts to end the religious schism between East and West in hopes that Christian union might save the empire

1440 Belgrade is unsuccessfully besieged by the Turks

1449 Constantine XI Dragases, last of the Byzantine emperors, begins his four-year reign

1452 The Turks build the fortress Remeli Hisar, closing the Bosporus to Christian invaders

1453 Constantinople is besieged by Mehmet II and at last falls to the Turks, ending the Byzantine empire

BIBLIOGRAPHY

These books were selected during the preparation of this volume for their interest and authority, and for their usefulness to readers seeking additional information on specific points.

An asterisk (*) marks works available in both hard-cover and paperback editions; a dagger (†) indicates availability only in paperback.

ART AND ARCHITECTURE

Ainalov, D. V., *The Hellenistic Origins of Byzantium.* Transl. by S. X. B. Hartley. Rutgers University Press, 1961.
Beckwith, John, *The Art of Constantinople.* Phaidon, 1961.
Bihalji-Merin, Oto, *Byzantine Frescoes and Icons in Yugoslavia.* Abrams, 1958.
Bovini, Giuseppe, *Ravenna Mosaics.* New York Graphic Society, 1956.
†Chatzidakis, Manolis and André Grabar, *Byzantine and Early Medieval Painting.* Compass, 1966.
†Constable, W. G., *The Painters' Workshop.* Beacon Paperbacks, 1963.
Demus, Otto, *Byzantine Mosaic Decoration.* Kegan Paul Trench Trubner, London, 1947.
Demus, Otto, and Ernst Diez, *Byzantine Mosaics in Greece.* Harvard University Press, 1931.
Grabar, André, *Byzantine Painting.* Skira, 1953.
Krautheimer, Richard, *Early Christian and Byzantine Architecture.* Penguin, 1965.
Larousse Encyclopedia of Byzantine and Medieval Art. René Huyghe, ed., G. P. Putnam, 1963.
Michelis, P. A., *An Aesthetic Approach to Byzantine Art.* Batsford, 1964.
Morey, C. R., *Christian Art.* W. W. Norton, 1958.
Rice, David Talbot, *Art of the Byzantine Era.* Frederick A. Praeger, 1963.
Rice, David Talbot, *The Art of Byzantium.* Henry N. Abrams, 1959.
Rice, David Talbot, *Masterpieces of Byzantine Art.* Aldine, 1958.
Simpson's History of Early Christian, Byzantine and Romanesque Architecture, Vol. II. Cecil Stewart, ed., Longmans, 1962.
†Thompson, Daniel V., *The Materials and Techniques of Medieval Painting.* Dover, 1957.
Volbach, W. F., and Max Hirmer, *Early Christian Art: The Late Roman and Byzantine Empires from the Third to the Seventh Century.* Henry N. Abrams, 1962.
Weitzmann, Kurt, *Greek Mythology in Byzantine Art.* Princeton University Press, 1951.

GEOGRAPHY

*Fox, Edward Whiting, ed., *Atlas of European History.* Oxford University Press, 1964.
†McEvedy, Colin, *The Penguin Atlas of Medieval History.* Penguin, 1961.
Shepherd, William R., *Historical Atlas.* Barnes & Noble, 1964.
Van Der Meer, F., and Christine Mohrmann, *Atlas of the Early Christian World.* Thomas Nelson, 1959.

GENERAL HISTORY

Baynes, Norman H., *Byzantine Studies and Other Essays.* Oxford University Press, 1960.
Baynes, Norman H., *The Byzantine Empire.* Oxford University Press, 1958.
†Baynes, Norman H.,and Henry St. L. B. Moss, eds., *Byzantium: An Introduction to East Roman Civilization.* Oxford at the Clarendon Press, 1962.
†Bury, J. B., *History of the Later Roman Empire,* 2 vols. Dover, 1958.
Byron, Robert, *Byzantine Achievement.* Russell & Russell, 1964.
The Cambridge Medieval History, Vol. IV, *Byzantine Empire.* Cambridge University Press, 1966.
Choukas, Michael, *Black Angels of Athos.* Stephen Daye, 1934.
Diehl, Charles, *Byzantine Empresses.* Transl. by Harold Bell and Theresa de Kerpely. Alfred A. Knopf, 1963.
Diehl, Charles, *Byzantium, Greatness and Decline.* Transl. by Naomi Walford. Rutgers University Press, 1957.
Diehl, Charles, *Byzantine Portraits.* Transl. by Harold Bell. Alfred A. Knopf, 1927.
Diehl, Charles, *History of the Byzantine Empire.* Transl. by George B. Ives. Princeton University Press, 1945.

Downey, Glanville, *Constantinople in the Age of Justinian.* University of Oklahoma Press, 1960.
Dvornick, Frances, *The Slavs in European History.* Rutgers University Press, 1962.
Every, George, *The Byzantine Patriarchate.* Seabury, 1962.
Gibbon, Edward, *The Decline and Fall of the Roman Empire: 80 A.D.-395 A.D.* 3 vols. Modern Library, 1966.
Hayes, Carleton J. H., *History of Western Civilization.* Macmillan, 1962.
†Hitti, Philip K., *The History of the Arabs.* St. Martin's, 1963.
†Hussey, John M., *The Byzantine World.* Harper Torchbooks, 1961.
†Lemerle, Paul, *A History of Byzantium.* Walker, 1964.
Liddell, Robert, *Byzantium and Istanbul.* Lawrence Verry, 1958.
Lindsay, Jack, *Byzantium into Europe.* Humanities, 1952.
Ostrogorsky, George, *History of the Byzantine State.* Transl. by Joan Hussey. Rutgers University Press, 1957.
Procopius, *History of the Wars.* 7 vols. Transl. by H. B. Dewing. Loeb Classical Library, 1961.
*Procopius, *Secret History.* Transl. by Richard Atwater. University of Michigan Press, 1961.
Rice, David Talbot, *The Byzantines.* Thames & Hudson, 1962.
Rice, David Talbot, and W. Swaan, *Constantinople, from Byzantium to Istanbul.* Stein & Day, 1965.
Rice, David Talbot, *Dark Ages.* Thames & Hudson, 1965.
*Runciman, Steven, *A History of the Crusades.* 3 vols. Cambridge University Press, 1954.
*Runciman, Steven, *Byzantine Civilization.* St. Martin's, 1966.
Runciman, Steven, *The Fall of Constantinople, 1453.* Cambridge University Press, 1965.
Stewart, Cecil, *Byzantine Legacy.* G. Allen & Unwin, London, 1949.
†Vasiliev, A. A., *History of the Byzantine Empire: 324-1453.* 2 vols. University of Wisconsin Press, 1964.
*White, Lynn, Jr., *Medieval Technology and Social Change.* Oxford at the Clarendon Press, 1962.

MILITARY HISTORY

Anderson, R. C., *Oared Fighting Ships.* Percival Marshall, London, 1962.
Mitchell, Colonel William A., *Outlines of the World's Military History.* Military Service Publishing Company, 1940.
Montross, Lynn, *War through the Ages.* Harper & Brothers, 1960.
*Oman, Charles, *A History of War in the Middle Ages.* 2 vols. Burt Franklin, 1924.
Payne-Gallway, Sir Ralph, *The Crossbow.* The Holland Press, London, 1964.
Toy, Sidney, *A History of Fortification from 3000 B.C. to A.D. 1700.* William Heinemann, Ltd., London, 1955.

RELIGION AND PHILOSOPHY

†Benz, Ernst, *The Eastern Orthodox Church: Its Thought and Life.* Transl. by Richard and Clara Winston. Anchor, 1963.
French, R. M., *The Eastern Orthodox Church.* Hutchinson's University Library, 1951.
Sherrard, Philip, *Constantinople: Iconography of a Sacred City.* Oxford University Press, 1965.
Sherrard, Philip, *Athos, the Mountain of Silence.* Oxford University Press, 1960.
†Ware, Timothy, *The Orthodox Church.* Penguin, 1963.
Zernov, Nicolas, *Eastern Christendom: A Study and Development of the Eastern Orthodox Church.* G. P. Putnam, 1961.

ART INFORMATION AND PICTURE CREDITS

The sources for the illustrations in this book are set forth below. Descriptive notes on the works of art are included. Credits for pictures positioned from left to right are separated by semicolons, from top to bottom by dashes. Photographers' names which follow a descriptive note appear in parentheses. Abbreviations include "c." for century and "ca." for circa.

Cover—St. Demetrios, mosaic detail from the Church of Hosios Loukas, Phocis, Greece, mid–11th c. (Erich Lessing from Magnum).

CHAPTER 1: 10—Shroud of St. Germain l'Auxerrois, silk, 9th c., Church of St. Eusebius, Auxerre, France (Eric Schaal). 15—Personifications of Rome and Constantinople, ivory diptych, 5th c., Kunsthistorisches Museum, Vienna (Photo Emile). 17—Martyrdom of St. Domninus, manuscript illumination from the *Menologion* of Basil II, Vatican Ms. Grec. 1613, page 78, 979-984, Vatican Library, Rome (Dmitri Kessel). 19—Dream of Constantine and Battle of Milvian Bridge, detail of manuscript illumination from the *Homilies* of St. Gregory of Nazianzus, Ms. grec. 510, folio 440, 867-886, Bibliothèque Nationale, Paris. 20, 21—Justinian and his Court, mosaic from the Church of San Vitale, Ravenna, Italy, 526-547 (Dmitri Kessel); Manuscript page from introduction to the *Code of Justinian*, Pandette c. 16, late 6th c., Biblioteca Medicea-Laurenziana, Florence, Italy. 22, 23 —Assumption of the Virgin Mary, manuscript illumination from the *Sermons* of James of Kokkinobaphos, Ms. grec. 1208, folio 3 verso, 12th c., Bibliothèque Nationale, Paris (Courtesy Thames and Hudson, Ltd., London); Old façade of St. Mark's, lunette mosaic from the Duomo di San Marco, Venice, Italy, 1260-1270 (Dmitri Kessel)—Bronze horses from the Duomo di San Marco, Venice, Italy, 4th-3rd c. B.C. (Dmitri Kessel). 24, 25—Relics of the Passion in Constantinople's Churches, manuscript illumination from *Le Livre des Merveilles*, Ms. fran. 2810, folio 144, ca. 1410, Bibliothèque Nationale, Paris;

Cross of Justin II, silver gilt on later gold base, 565-578, Tesoro di San Pietro, Vatican, Rome (Dmitri Kessel). 26, 27—Detail from the Death of St. Ephraim the Syrian, panel painting by Emmanuel Tzanphournaris of Crete, 16th c., Pinacoteca Vaticana, Rome (Emmett Bright); Goreme, Turkey (Farrell Grehan from Photo Researchers). 28, 29—Baptism of the Bulgarians, manuscript illumination from Bulgarian copy of the *Chronicle* of Constantine Manasses, Vatican Codex Slav. 2, folio 163 verso, 1345, Vatican Library, Rome (Courtesy Thames and Hudson, Ltd., London); Three Holy Children in the Fiery Furnace, fresco from Faras, Sudan, 10th-11th c., Courtesy Prof. K. Michalowski, Warsaw, Director of Polish Excavations at Faras (Dr. Georg Gerster from Rapho Guillumette).

CHAPTER 2: 30—Constantine presenting Constantinople to the Virgin, mosaic detail from Hagia Sophia, 986-994 (Dmitri Kessel). 35—Reliquary casket (?), ivory relief, 6th-7th c., Cathedral Treasury of Trier, Germany (Foto, Museum of the Bishopric of Trier). 39—Clephane Horn, ivory, 10th-11th c., Courtesy of the Trustees of the British Museum, London. 41, 44-53—Drawings by Paul Hogarth.

CHAPTER 3: 54—St. George, steatite relief, 12th c., Treasury of Vatopedi, Mount Athos, Greece (Dmitri Kessel). 63-73—Manuscript illuminations from the *Chronicle* of John Scylitzes, Matritensis graecus, Vitr. 26-2 [63—folio 156. 64, 65—folio 82 verso; folio 82—folio 84; folio 83. 66, 67—folio 85 verso; folio 85; folio 86—folio 86. 68—folio 87 verso—folio 87—folio 80. 69—folio 80 verso—folio 80 verso—folio 102. 70, 71—folio 99 verso—folio 100; folio 98 verso. 72—folio 104 verso—folio 105 verso—folio 105 verso. 73—folio 104 verso; folio 105—folio 102.] 14th c., Biblioteca Nacional, Madrid (Augusto Meneses).

CHAPTER 4: 74—Emperor John Cantacuzenoe and the Council of 1351, manuscript illumination from the "Manuscript of Cantacuzenoe," Ms. grec. 1242, folio 5 verso, 1370-75, Bibliothèque Nationale, Paris (Eric Schaal). 76—Head of Nicephoras Phocas, manuscript illumination from the *Chronicle* of John Scylitzes, Matritensis graecus, Vitr. 26-2, folio 157 verso, 14th c., Biblioteca Nacional, Madrid (Augusto Meneses). 78—Empress Theodora, mosaic detail from the Church of San Vitale, Ravenna, Italy, 526-547 (Dmitri Kessel); Empress Zoë, mosaic detail from Hagia Sophia, 1028-1042 (Dmitri Kessel); Empress Irene, mosaic detail from Hagia Sophia, ca. 1118-1122 (Dmitri Kessel). 81—Crowning of David, manuscript illumination from the *Paris Psalter*, Ms. grec. 139, folio 6 verso, early 10th c., Bibliothèque Nationale, Paris. 83—Imperial cavalry, detail of manuscript illumination from the *Chronicle* of John Scylitzes, Matritensis graecus, Vitr. 26-2, folio 54 verso, 14th c., Biblioteca Nacional, Madrid (Augusto Meneses). 84—Mounted hunter, detail from ivory casket, 11th c., Cathedral Treasury of Troyes, France (Eddy Van der Veen)—Drawings by David Klein. 85—St. Demetrios, steatite relief, 12th c., Courtesy Marquis Hubert de Ganay, Paris (Sabine Weiss from Rapho Guillumette)—Drawings by David Klein. 86—Drawings by David Klein. 87—Manuscript illuminations from the *Book of Machines of War* of Heron of Byzantium, Vatican Codex Grec. 1605 [folio 8 verso—folio 9 verso; folio 20 recto—folio 40 recto], mid-11th c., Vatican Library, Rome. 88, 89—Manuscript illumination from the *Book of Machines of War* of Heron of Byzantium, Vatican Codex Grec. 1605, folio 36 recto, mid-11th c., Vatican Library, Rome; Drawing by David Klein based on a model in The Naval Museum, Piraeus, Greece. 90-91—Map of Constantinople, Florentine manuscript illumination from the *Liber insularum archipelagi* of Cristoforo Buondelmonti, Ms. Cotton Vespasian A XIII, folio 36 verso, ca. 1422, Courtesy of the Trustees of the British Museum, London; Drawing by David Klein.

CHAPTER 5: 92—Emperor Nicephoras Botaniates between St. John Chrysostom and the Archangel Michael, manuscript illumination from the *Homilies* of St. John Chrysostom, Ms. grec. Coislin 79, folio 2 verso, ca. 1078, Bibliothèque Nationale, Paris. 95—Maitreya Buddha, Chinese bronze gilt statue, 477, The Metropolitan Museum of Art, New York, Kennedy Fund, 1926. 99—St. Simeon Stylites, manuscript illumination from the *Menologion* of Basil II, Vatican Ms. Grec. 1613, page 2, 979-984, Vatican Library, Rome (Dmitri Kessel). 101, 104-109—Mosaics from the Church of Hosios Loukas, Phocis, Greece, mid-11th c. (Erich Lessing from Magnum). 102, 103—Floor plan and elevation by Lowell Hess after R. W. Schultz and S. H. Barnsley, *The Monastery of St. Luke of Stiris in Phocis*, London, Macmillan & Co. 110, 111—Pantocrator, mosaic detail from the dome of the Church of the Virgin, Daphni, Greece, late 11th c. (Erich Lessing from Magnum).

CHAPTER 6: 112—Canticle of Moses, manuscript illumination from the *Septuagint*, Vatican Codex Grec. 752, folio 449 verso, 11th c., Vatican Library, Rome. 115—Gold necklace from the Cyprus Treasure, 6th-7th c., The Metropolitan Museum of Art, New York, Gift of J. Pierpont Morgan, 1917. 117—Bezant of Emperor Constantine VII Porphyrogenitus, 945, British Museum (Derek Bayes). 119-133—Photographs of Olympos, Greece (Constantine Manos from Magnum). 120—Byzantine Imperial Eagle, manuscript illumination from Sinai Codex Gr. 2123, folio 133 recto, 15th-16th c., Monastery of St. Catherine, Mount Sinai, Egypt, Courtesy of the Mount Sinai Expeditions sponsored by the University of Michigan, Princeton University and the University of Alexandria (Fred Anderegg). 122—Woman with Spindle, manuscript illumination from the *Book of Job*, Ms. grec. 134, folio 184 verso, 13th c., Bibliothèque Nationale, Paris (Eric Schaal). 129—Christ crowning Romanus and Eudoxia, ivory relief, ca. 950, Cabinet des Médailles, Bibliothèque Nationale, Paris.

CHAPTER 7: 134—Praglia Abbey, Padua, Italy (Emmett Bright). 137—Hymn of Casia from Codex Dalassenos, Codex Vindobensis Theologicus Grecus 181, folio 232 verso, 12th c., Österreichische Nationalbibliothek, Vienna, Austria—Art work by Nicholas Fasciano after Egon Wellesz, *A History of Byzantine Music and Hymnography*, Oxford, Clarendon Press, 1962 and H. J. W. Tillyard, "Handbook of the Middle Byzantine Notation," *Monumenta Musicae Byzantinae Subsidia*, Vol. 1, fasc. i, Copenhagen, Levin and Munksgaard, 1935—Neume system by Edward Roesner after Wellesz and Tillyard. 139—Drawings by Nicholas Fasciano after Cecil Stewart, *Byzantine Legacy*, London, George Allen & Unwin, Ltd., 1947. 142—Veroli Casket, gilded ivory panels, 10th c., Victoria and Albert Museum, London. 145—Pantocrator, Church of St. Savior in Chora, Istanbul, 1300-1320 (Dmitri Kessel). 146-147—Three Holy Children in the Fiery Furnace, mosaic from the Church of Hosios Loukas, Phocis, Greece, mid-11th c. (Erich Lessing from Magnum). 148, 149—Christ Enthroned, mosaic detail from the Basilica of Sant' Apollinare Nuovo, Ravenna, Italy, early 6th c. (Aldo Durazzi); Christ Enthroned, mosaic detail from the Zoë Panel in Hagia Sophia, 1028-42 (Dmitri Kessel); Christ Enthroned, mosaic detail from the Deesis Panel in Hagia Sophia, ca. 1280 (Dmitri Kessel). 150—Detail of gold cemetery glass from the Catacombs, 4th c., Vatican Library, Rome (Dmitri Kessel); Detail of mosaic from the Mausoleum of Galla Placidia, Ravenna, Italy, early 5th c. (Dmitri Kessel)—Detail of encaustic wax panel painting, 7th c., Monastery of St. Catherine, Mount Sinai, Egypt (Roger Wood Studio); Detail of ivory triptych, 10th c., Palazzo Venezia, Rome (Emmett Bright)—Detail of the Pala d'Oro, cloisonné enamel plaque, 12th c., Duomo di San Marco, Venice, Italy (Emmett Bright); Detail of fresco by Eutychius and Michael, from the Church of St. Clement, Ohrid, Yugoslavia, ca. 1295 (Sonja Bullaty and Angelo Lomeo). 151—Detail of mosaic from the Church of the Virgin, Daphni, Greece, late 11th c. (Eric Schaal)—Portable icon, mosaic of miniature tesserae set in wax, from the Church of St. Mary Pammakaristos, Istanbul, 12th c., Collection of the Ecumenical Patriarchate of Constantinople (Ara Guler)—Detail of fresco in the Pareccleseion of the Church of St. Savior in Chora, Istanbul, ca. 1303 (Ara Guler). 152, 153—Barberini Ivory, ivory relief, early 6th c., Musée du Louvre, Paris (Giraudon, Paris); Harbaville Triptych, ivory relief, late 10th c., Musée du Louvre, Paris (Service Photographique de la Réunion des Musées Nationaux). 154—David Composing the Psalms, manuscript illumination from the *Paris Psalter*, Ms. grec. 139, folio 1 verso, early 10th c., Bibliothèque Nationale, Paris. 155—Christ Teaching, manuscript illumination from the *Menologion* of Basil II, Vatican Codex Grec. 1613, page 1, 979-984, Vatican Library, Rome (Dmitri Kessel)—St. Eumenius, manuscript illumination from the *Menologion* of Basil II, Vatican Codex Grec. 1613, page 47, 979-984, Vatican Library, Rome (Dmitri Kessel). 156, 157—Apse and Semi-dome, fresco by Eutychius and Michael, from the Church of St. Clement, Ohrid, Yugoslavia, ca. 1295 (Sonja Bullaty and Angelo Lomeo). 158—David Presented to Saul, silver plate from the Cyprus Treasure, early 7th c., The Metropolitan Museum of Art, New York, Gift of J. Pierpont Morgan, 1917—The Annunciation, silk twill, 7th-8th c., Vatican Library, Rome (Dmitri Kessel). 159—Outer container for reliquary of the True Cross, enameled gold inlaid with jewels, ca. 955-960, Cathedral Treasury of Limburg on the Lahn, Germany (Hirmer-Fotoarchiv München).

CHAPTER 8: 160—Siege of Constantinople, manuscript illumination from the *Voyage d'Outremer* of Bertrandon de la Brocquière, Ms. fran. 9087, folio 207 verso, 1455, Bibliothèque Nationale, Paris. 169—Sultan Mehmet II, oil painting by Gentile Bellini of Venice, 1480, The National Gallery, London, Reproduced by courtesy of the Trustees (Culver Pictures). 171—Monastery of St. John the Evangelist, Patmos, Greece (Dmitri Kessel). 172, 173—Monastery of St. Catherine, Mount Sinai, Egypt (Dr. Georg Gerster from Rapho Guillumette). 174, 175—Convent of Roussanou, Meteora, Greece (Dmitri Kessel); Mount Athos, Greece (Dmitri Kessel)—Great Lavra, Mount Athos, Greece (Dmitri Kessel). 176—Photograph by Dmitri Kessel. 177—Monastery of St. John the Evangelist, Patmos, Greece (Dmitri Kessel). 178, 179—Dionysiou Monastery, Mount Athos, Greece (Dmitri Kessel). 180, 181—Mount Athos, Greece (John Marmaras from Black Star of London).

ACKNOWLEDGMENTS

The editors of this book are particularly indebted to Peter Charanis, Voorhees Professor of History, Rutgers, The State University, New Jersey; Josepha Weitzmann-Fiedler; Ronald E. Malmstrom; Evangelos Savvopoulos, Minister to the Prime Minister's Office, Athens; John Kondis, General Director of Archaeology, Athens; Manolis Chatzidakis, Director of Byzantine and Benaki Museums, Athens; Paul Lazaridis, Curator of Byzantine Antiquities, Athens; Stella Papadaki, Assistant Director, and Nikos Zias, Byzantine Museum, Athens; Paul Mylonas, National Academy of Fine Arts, Athens; George Cavounides, Director-General of the Press Division of the Prime Minister's Office, Athens; Nicolas Linardatos, Director, Foreign Press Division, Athens; Francis R. Walton, Director, Gennadeion Library, Athens; Harry Hionides, Athens College, Athens; Simon Karas, Director of Ethnic Music of the Greek Radio; Vatican Library, Rome; Tullia Gasparrini Leporace, Director, Gian Albino Ravalli Modoni, Mario Favaretto, Biblioteca Marciana, Venice; Giuseppe Tamburrino, Abbazia di Praglia, Padua; Ferdinando Rodriquez, Biblioteca Universitaria, Bologna; Irma Merolle-Tondi, Director, Biblioteca Medicea-Laurenziana, Florence; Hirmer Verlag, Munich; Paul Gichtel, Bayerische Staatsbibliothek, Handschriften-Abteilung, Munich; Bildarchiv Foto Marburg; Rudolf Noll, Kunsthistorisches Museum, Vienna; Paul Lemerle, L'Institut d'Histoire et Civilization Byzantines, Paris; Françoise Le Monnier, Conservateur du Département de la Photographie, Bibliothèque Nationale, Paris; Department of British and Mediaeval Antiquities, British Museum, London; Manuscript Department, British Museum, London; Department of Western Manuscripts, The Bodleian Library, Oxford; Col. John R. Elting, U.S. Army; Fred Anderegg, Director of Photographic Services, University of Michigan; Ben Lieberman, Communications Consultant, New York; F. E. Peters, Department of Classics, New York University; Alexander Dunkel, Instructor of Russian Language and Literature, New York University; Edward Roesner, New York University; Kenneth Levy, Woolworth Center of Musical Studies, Princeton University; the Rev. Leonidas C. Contos, Dean, and the Rev. Demetrios Constantelos of the Holy Cross Greek Orthodox Theological School, Brookline, Massachusetts; the Rev. John Maheras, Greek Orthodox Archdiocese of North and South America, New York.

INDEX

x

PRODUCTION STAFF FOR TIME INCORPORATED

John L. Hallenbeck (Vice President and Director of Production),
Robert E. Foy, Caroline Ferri and Robert E. Fraser
Text photocomposed under the direction of Albert J. Dunn and Arthur J. Dunn